"From his experiences as a P [   ] leper colonies to his experiences as a writer and speaker for Zig Ziglar's 'Born to Win' conferences, Dr. Gallagher invites you, through his book *Burning: Passionate Prayers for Men on Fire*, to join his army of courageous leaders and prayer warriors. This is your opportunity to seize the many ways to improve YOURSELF, your FAMILY, your COMMUNITY, your CHURCH, and your NATION."

—Ray Fulenwider
National Church Growth Consultant
and author, *The Servant-Driven Church*

"Dr. Gallagher possesses a clear vision of grace, liberty, and the opportunity to do the work of God that God calls us to do. You will find his book, *Burning: Passionate Prayers for Men on Fire*, challenging, inspirational, and instructional."

—William Banowsky, PhD
President (former), Pepperdine University and
University of Oklahoma

Burning

Passionate Prayers® for Men on Fire

Burning

Passionate Prayers® for Men on Fire

Every Woman's Gift for
Every Man in Her Life

W. Neil Gallagher, PhD

"Next to the Bible, every man needs to read *Burning* every morning."
—Frank Reed, Morning Host, KLTY-America's #1 Christian Station

BROWN
CHRISTIAN PRESS

Burning: Passionate Prayers for Men on Fire
Every Woman's Gift for Every Man in Her Life

Brown Christian Press
16250 Knoll Trail Drive, Suite 205
Dallas, Texas 75248
www.BrownBooks.com
(972) 381-0009

A New Era in Publishing™

ISBN 978-1-61254-166-2
LCCN 2014939274

Printed in the United States

10 9 8 7 6 5 4 3 2 1

For more information or to contact the author, please go to
www.BurningPassionatePrayers.com

Dedicated to George Mueller, David Wilkerson, William Booth, and Randall Terry, whose fiery prayers and compassionate actions have rescued millions.

All in One

Passionate Prayers

Personal Devotional

Bible Study

"I want the world to know that I am a man **burning** for you."

—**Toby Mac**
Christian Rapper, Grammy Award Winner

"I had a hot heart for God and a **passionate burning within me.** My hot heart for God was greater than my talent for God. If your heart burns for God, you will build a great life."

—**John Maxwell, PhD**
Leadership Expert, *New York Times* Best-Selling Author

*I have listened to you, and received, your ever-so **passionate prayers**.*

—**1 Kings 9:3**

In the sixth year, in the sixth month on the fifth day, while I was sitting in my house and the *elders* of Judah were sitting before me, the hand of the Sovereign Lord came on me there. *I looked, and I saw a figure like that of a man. From what appeared to be his waist down he **was like fire**, and from there up his appearance was as bright as glowing metal.*

—**Ezekiel 8:1**

Some people teach about authentic Christian living;

some people write about authentic Christian living;

other people live it.

You seized this book.
You're number three.

Contents

Burning for Family

Burning for Others

Burning to Grow

Burning for America

Prologue

Hey, guys, let's prove them wrong. Let's show the world that we've got passionate purpose, especially in our prayers.

"Dr. Gallagher, you're CRAZY to write this book. You're wasting time, energy, and paper. Men don't read books!"

Really?

Maybe that's true for the indecisive and uncommitted. But that's not you.

You're a man's man and a woman's hero.

You picked this up.

You're a player.

You're burning

- to glorify God,
- to love your family,
- to encourage others,
- to grow in muscle and mind, and
- to enrich, protect, and preserve America.

Better yet, you've had a loving woman give you this book: your wife, mother, sister, daughter, grandmother, or special friend. A woman who sees the leader in you.

That's another reason you'll embrace this book and you will pass it on.

You really are a man's man, and a woman's hero. You're burning with love, courage, compassion, gratitude, and purpose.

You are fired up, ready to lead both men and women.

Leaders can't lead until they've learned to bow before the One who leads them. Your God, your family, the people in your church, your employees and your customers, and the people of this country need you to lead, but they first need you to pray—passionately, boldly, and daily. They need you to be set ablaze with Isaiah's fire and to burn in your passion for God.

Burning is not a book designed merely to inspire. It is an inferno to ignite action, releasing your passion for God.

Grab each chapter like a torch. Use the sections at the end of each chapter to record your thoughts. Listen to what God says to you in your prayer time. Follow the scripture passages to guide your study. Blast off.

Burning for God

1

Burning to Worship

Lord, for years I fought worship.

Worship *who*, I asked?

How do I surrender to the invisible? My university professors told me that touch, taste, smell, sight, and sound are all that can be known. Oh, and of course, reason.

Empiricism and rationalism rule. What's to worship with that?

I read that worship means I express words or sing songs or perform actions, which show that another is well, worthy.

Worthier than I. Bigger, better, stronger, and smarter than I.

Worship acknowledges: "God, you're great and I'm not."

Still I struggled.

Lord, you know how I believed back then that I was the source of my happiness and the center of my significance. I recognized nothing higher.

But what a difference your Book made. Thank you for your patience.

Remember, Lord? I read it back then to prove that you and your followers were wrong. Then you opened my mind, and I studied it again.

Open heart plus open mind will always get cha'.

With your guidance, I learned the relief, release, and joy of worship. I learned the TRUTH. Now my heart burns for worship because of you.

Thank you, Lord.

I now lay myself flat and bury my nose in the carpet before you. I slam my knees to the tile and shut my eyes in silence to absorb your love. I raise both arms and open my hands like when I do the wave at the ballpark: my wave of worship to you. I worship you.

Lord, I was dumb to fight worship for so long. To give myself to worship seemed "out of control." I told my college buddies what I had found in your Book. I told them the joy I found in being *born again*.

"Gallagher has finally lost it. He has gone off the deep end," they sneered.

Yet with the clarity of mind you offered me, Lord, I now ask the question: "Isn't the deep end for those who have no roads and no rules?"

If

    a) you don't know where you're going and

    b) there are no road signs and

c) there are no driving rules . . . aren't you the one likely to stumble into a deep ditch and

    roll,

        roll,

            roll

                down to destruction?

Isn't the deep end for those who are deeply into themselves?

Thank you, Lord, that unlike a tree, rock, fish, or dog, I can love you as Creator and know that you love me. Since my surrender, Lord, in worship and work, you have delighted me with six words: I WANT THE BEST FOR YOU. Thank you, Lord.

I worship you, Lord, because you are worthy. I fall to my face and sink to my knees. Only you are worthy to receive my acts of surrender and service and praise. I want to show you daily what you are worth to me. Amen.

The Flame:

Exalt the LORD our God and worship at his footstool; he is holy.

Psalm 99:5

But I, by your great mercy, will come into your house; in reverence will I bow down toward your holy temple.

Psalm 5:7

God is spirit, and his worshipers must worship in spirit and in truth.

John 4:24

FIRE IT UP!

How I worship (Write down ways you express worship.):

_____

_____

_____

_____

_____

_____

_____

My Passionate Prayer Time (Write down areas you desire to bring to the Lord in prayer.):

_____

_____

_____

_____

_____

_____

_____

_____

2

Burning for the Church

We don't do church anymore.

Lord, I didn't say that. That was Michael who just left my office. He and his family, well, they went to a Catholic church and found out that the priest was busted for molesting altar boys.

Forget that.

So they went to a small Bible church and learned that the preacher was sleeping with a pretty neighbor.

Forget that too.

"Dr. Gallagher, we just don't do church anymore."

I hadn't thought of it at the time, Lord, but help me to keep your perspective in view:

> *Peter turned and saw that the disciple whom*
> *Jesus loved was following them. (This was the one*

who had leaned back against Jesus at the supper and had said, "Lord, who is going to betray you?") When Peter saw him, he asked, "Lord, what about him?"

Jesus answered, "If I want him to remain alive until I return, what is that to you? You must follow me."

John 21:20–22

You follow me.

Those are your words, Lord. I want to obey you.

But there are four ways I need for you to help me:

First, remind me, Lord, lovingly and frequently to say to the Michaels of the world that following you is a personal decision, regardless of what others decide about you. You hold me accountable for my life and for what I choose to believe and how passionately I determine to follow you. I need to remember that. And I need you, Lord, to remind me to say that to others who are struggling.

Second, help me to encourage people not to be distracted by the so-called *hypocrites* in the church with the understanding that no one is perfect, except you. You are always the same, yesterday, today, and for all time. I want people to know you and that you will never let them down, Lord.

I will embrace the billboard message I saw in Perry, Georgia: ". . . don't let a phony Christian keep you from Jesus Christ."

Third, help me to remind Michael and others like him that the church is a hospital for sinners. In fact, you said yourself, "It is not the healthy who need a doctor but the sick." That makes perfect sense. People who think of themselves as perfect and in no need of you are mistaken.

Fourth, Lord, help me to share with the Michaels of the world that we "do" church because other people need us. Hurting people need others to help lift them out of fear, to help free them from patterns of worry, to walk with them through their depression and loneliness, and ultimately, to lead them away from self-destruction. Your church, Lord, is a metaphor for unconditional love and is a haven for people who are hurting. The church is the body of Christ and is the only genuine place where one can find a living hope, a strength in weakness, and the promise of lifelong deliverance.

Lord, I respect businesses and educators, so I am not criticizing anybody, but IBM will never bring salvation. General Electric cannot heal a broken family. Wal-Mart has no power to deliver someone from the curse of sin. Coca-Cola® will not heal a guilty conscience, and Harvard and Stanford can never "be sin for us, so that in him we might become the righteousness of God" (2 Cor. 5:21). That's what you did for me and for Michael, Lord. And for everyone who follows you.

Big corporations, big government, big education do not heal the human condition. So, Lord, when you hear Michael say, "Deliver me from church," remind him through me that you need him to stay because other people need him and because he needs you. And you are in the church, lovingly expressed through the people you have redeemed. Finally, ignite in me the fire, Lord, to go to church eager to learn from the lips of godly pastors and teachers and to help others at church to conquer this daily adventure we call *life*. And help me inspire the Michaels of the world to "do church" with the same passion.

The Flame:

Let us not give up meeting together, as some are in the habit of doing, but let us encourage one another—and all the more as you see the Day approaching.

Hebrews 10:25

To the church of the firstborn, whose names are written in heaven. You have come to God, the judge of all men, to the spirits of righteous men made perfect.

Hebrews 12:23

FIRE IT UP!

These are the reasons I want to be in church:

_____

_____

_____

_____

_____

_____

_____

_____

My Passionate Prayer Time:

_____

_____

_____

_____

_____

_____

_____

_____

3

Burning to Praise You

Lord, I see the picture now. Praising you is like the astronauts in their space capsule en route to the moon. They float freely in space because they have no pressure. They rise above the earth.

That's what happens to me, Lord, when I praise you. I rise above the earth and all life's worries, demands, disappointments, and pressures.

I am free of worry when my mind is focused on praising you. Your word gives me lift.

I will praise You, Lord, with all my heart;

I will bow down toward your holy temple and will praise your name for your love and faithfulness, for you have so exalted your solemn decree that it surpasses your fame.

When I called, you answered me; You greatly emboldened me.

Though I walk in the midst of trouble, you preserve my life; You stretch out your hand against the anger of my foes, with your right hand you save me.

Psalms 138:1, 2, 3, and 7

That says it all, doesn't it, Lord?

I praise you because you have revealed yourself and your Law (v. 2).

I praise you because you respond to me (v. 3).

I praise you because you revive and redeem me (v. 7).

I also praise you for your mighty acts, Lord:

- the creation of the world
- the creation of my body
- the creation of my spirit.

I praise you with raised hands and exuberant voice. I praise you because I am the object of your countless thoughts and deepest affection.

I praise you that you are not a stone or a tree. You are a person moved by my prayers, appreciative of my motives, and dedicated to fulfilling only good in my life. I praise you that you do not manipulate me. You honor my free will.

I praise you for an array of environs:

- desert and mountain

- ocean and forest
- arctic and tropical.

I praise you that you have adopted me as your child, knowing that an adopted child is twice loved.

I praise you that you have revealed yourself to all of us as

- God, the Father. You are God above us.
- God, the Son Jesus. You are God with us.
- God, the Holy Spirit. You are God in us.

I praise you for in your overflowing plan, the more I praise you, the closer I am drawn to you and learn more reasons to praise you.

I praise you because you know I am not perfect. So you enacted the great exchange:

> *God made him who had no sin to be sin for us,*
> *so that in him we might become the righteousness*
> *of God.*
>
> 2 Corinthians 5:21

I praise you because you have given me faith in the future, knowing that faith in the future delivers power in the present.

I praise you that your unfailing love is our hope.

> *The Lord is good to those whose hope is in him, to*
> *the one who seeks him.*
>
> Lamentations 3:25

*But the eyes of the Lord are on those who fear
him, on those whose hope is in his unfailing love.*

Psalm 33:18

I praise you that your law is noble, dependable, rational, and universal. There is no guesswork, no popular vote on what is right or wrong.

I praise you for your law.

I praise you because in your light we see light. And I praise you because your light heals, exposes, warms, regenerates, and gives birth to all who believe.

I praise you, Lord, that your Son Jesus is the light of the world that overcomes spiritual darkness.

I praise you, Lord, because you are greater than my problems. I praise you because I am your workmanship created for good works that you have prepared for me.

*For we are God's workmanship, created in Christ
Jesus to do good works, which God prepared in
advance for us to do.*

Ephesians 2:10

I praise you for your assurance of peace.

*You will keep in perfect peace him whose mind is
steadfast, because he trusts in you.*

Isaiah 26:3

I praise you that I cannot fully experience you with my eyes or my ears. I know that sight and sound—and other senses—are variable and unreliable.

I praise you that I know you with a certainty of your Spirit speaking to mine.

I praise you that you have shown me that I do not wrestle against flesh and blood but against the rulers of darkness who are determined to destroy me and others. I praise you that I can claim your power and resist the Devil, and then watch him flee from me! I say, "Get thee behind me," and he bolts.

I praise you for your truth that, "He who is in me (Your Holy Spirit) is greater than he (Satan), who is in the world."

I praise you for your promise of ultimate goodness in my life as I put my trust in you.

The Flame:

Ascribe to the Lord the glory due His name; worship the Lord in the splendor of his holiness.

Psalm 29:2

And we know that in all things God works for the good of those who love him, who have been called according to his purpose.

Romans 8:28

FIRE IT UP!

Here are some things for which I praise you, Lord:

_____

_____

_____

_____

_____

_____

_____

_____

My Passionate Prayer Time:

_____

_____

_____

_____

_____

_____

_____

_____

4

Burning to be Unpopular

In fact, everyone who wants to live a godly life in
Christ Jesus will be persecuted.

2 Timothy 2:13

Lord, that's a tough one. You've got a lot of tough truths, but that's a *real* tough one. Lord, you know how easy it is for me to be drugged by likeability. I want to be understood, approved, appreciated, liked, and applauded. I don't want to be the object of anyone's anger. I don't want anyone to say, "You offended me." That hurts my feelings.

WAH!

Because I fear rejection, I often allow opportunities for teaching your word slip by.

When you give me an opportunity to speak of you, I want to shut up, fearing embarrassment or ridicule.

Remind me, Lord, of those times when you empowered me with compassion, conviction, and boldness to speak. Remember that day, Lord, when I was standing in the supermarket line? Three people in front, four in back. The lady right in front of me stood holding a baby. *This is it*, I said to myself. *Do it.*

"Beautiful baby!" I said.

At that point, the words of Lincoln resonated in my skull: "To sin by silence when we should speak up makes cowards of men."

"Oh, thank you, sir. She's a delight," she replied smiling.

And I said—real loud—"Can you imagine that there are people in the world that actually eliminate babies before they are born? Outrageous isn't it?"

Those in the front froze and listened. Those in the back froze and listened.

And I heard a couple of soft "Amens."

If there was anyone in that line who championed a woman's alleged right to kill her baby, they didn't speak up. The silence of the seven was profound.

Lord, your words of truth flowed through me and maybe, just maybe, changed the mind of an abortionist among the seven, and the drama that day certainly strengthened the pro-life convictions of all those within earshot.

How about that other time, Lord, when I was walking through Barnes & Noble? I saw that teen—a young, impressionable kid—reading a satanic novel. Though he wasn't my son, he was a teen you love and whose mind is so vulnerable.

I grabbed a Bible from an adjacent aisle, laid it in front of him, and said, "Hey, dude, this is a better read." He chuckled, teeth flashing above metal studs piercing his lips. He dropped Satan's book and picked up your book, Lord.

I love to remain comfortable, Lord, and I love to feel loved. But remind me of that amazing, hilarious paradox: Jesus was the most loved person who ever lived. Yet Jesus was the most hated person who ever lived too. Remind me of the value of taking risks, of speaking about you in spite of the fear of rejection.

Remind me that the only approval I ever need is yours, and that the approval of a family member, a church member, a co-worker, a boss, an important client, or a valued customer doesn't matter. Give me boldness to speak the truth because I love you and I love people.

Remind me, Lord, that your truth will set anyone free, but speaking your truth in love won't necessarily make me popular.

Also, remind me that the promotion of your love in *any setting* is positive, necessary, therapeutic, and potentially soul saving. Remind me to be the man you made me to be, not the man I'm often afraid to be.

Remind me that I love you enough to be open to your truths. When I pray, "Make my life a miracle of your service," I mean that, Lord. Remind me that if I really love people, I won't merely seek their approval but their improvement, redemption, healing, and salvation. I will seek to inspire courage in them to speak and to act for what is right, regardless of whether or not it's popular. Amen.

The Flame:

I am not ashamed of the gospel, because it is the power of God for the salvation of everyone who believes: first for the Jew, then for the Gentile.

Romans 1:16

Blessed are you when people insult you, persecute you and falsely say all kinds of evil against you because of me.

Matthew 5:11–12

FIRE IT UP!

This is how I am as "unpopular" as Jesus:

_____

_____

_____

_____

_____

_____

_____

_____

My Passionate Prayer Time:

_____

_____

_____

_____

_____

_____

_____

_____

5

Burning to Walk Across Niagara

Did you see that, Lord? Nik Wallenda just walked across Niagara Falls on a tight wire. He did it for you through your power and to encourage other people to dream big dreams. When you have big dreams, Wallenda says, and trust God and never give up, you will fulfill those dreams. I love that!

What a testimony he offered to the millions watching worldwide!

I want to walk with that simple trust; one step at a time—preparing, planning, and acting one step at a time. No matter how thick the mist or how violent the wind or how loud the skeptics, I want to be like Wallenda and just walk and walk and walk, fulfilling the goals you have for me.

Keep my eyes fixed on you and on the goals you have for me, Lord, and help me not to drown in the rushing waters of fear or faint under the roaring falls of doubt.

You also taught me long ago that I could drive all night in pitch darkness. All I needed was to see one hundred feet at a time guided by one hundred feet of light.

With your Word as my light and the power of your Spirit as an engine, I can drive all night through life down a road that is often dark and scary.

Keep my eyes fixed on my goals, Lord, that are actually your goals for me.

That's what I desire for my life, Lord.

Trusting you step by step, one hundred feet of road at a time. Amen.

The Flame:

And after he became the father of Methuselah, Enoch walked with God 300 years and had other sons and daughters. Altogether, Enoch lived 365 years. Enoch walked with God; then he was no more, because God took him away.

Genesis 5:22–24

Your word is a lamp to my feet and a light for my path.

Psalm 119:105

FIRE IT UP!

Here's how I choose to walk with God:

_____

_____

_____

_____

_____

_____

_____

_____

My Passionate Prayer Time:

_____

_____

_____

_____

_____

_____

_____

_____

6

Burning with the Anger of Jesus

Lord, by your grace and power, I REFUSE to be mad at

- The guy who cut me off. "I had the green light! And he still ran in front of me. Could have killed both of us."
- The relative who forgot my birthday.
- The repairman who left shards of glass on my welcome mat.
- The plumber guy who left water dripping from the ceiling.
- The medical secretary who got my billing wrong and won't return my calls.
- The gal who tapped my bumper in the store parking lot.

God, by your grace and power, I refuse to be mad at the people who interrupt my comfortable existence and cause me inconvenience.

I will lovingly hold people responsible for their behavior. I will demand accountability. I will insist on solutions and remedies.

But I will not surrender to that animal anger and rabid vengeance boiling on the streets of America.

I will not surrender to anger when I am hurt.

I will be righteously angry when innocent people, especially children, are hurt. That's what angered you, Lord—injustice.

And, like your Son Jesus, I will not be angry at people. Teach me to love sinners and hate the sin because I am a sinner too.

As Jesus was with the woman caught in adultery, I will shut my mouth when I am tempted to condemn.

Jesus refused to get angry when he himself was hurt or suffered mind-boggling injustice. He got angry when others were hurt, especially in the name of religion.

Jesus raged when his disciples kicked kids off his lap. He told his buddies, "Let the little children come to me. Don't shoo them away. Let them come to me."

To Jesus, all kids are hug hungry and extremely huggable. Jesus wants every child to feel the warmth of his Father's love. He still does. He wants that warmth in public schools and on playing fields. He rages when people or policies deny kids the opportunity to know him and experience his steadfast love.

When people hungry for God (in the temple that day) couldn't worship, Jesus raged because those in charge put rules around the rituals and barriers around the blessings. Jesus raged because God's people were being denied opportunities for worship and service. The only thing that flew higher than the doves that day was his blood racing to the tops of his ears.

You remember that time, Lord, when I testified before the zoning board of our town? The chairman said, "Dr. Gallagher, I don't understand. What's the big deal? They opened a Sweet Ecstasy adult bookstore next to the family shopping area. It's a free country. Why are you angry?"

"Why aren't *you*?" I asked the chairman.

I documented the facts about the devastating effects of pornography on marriages and families and explained the horrifying growth in human trafficking in America's cities as a result of this vicious industry. I showed them the stats and the dark, downward progression: how the *Playboy*-type magazines drive men to the sex-act magazines and then to explore and be enticed by child porn. The magazines and videos radiate the false image that women want to be raped, and that children enjoy being molested. That's the reason for rage.

The zoning law was changed—no Sweet Ecstasy bookstore.

God, let me burn with anger at the things that make you angry. And—for those events that merely "offend" me—let me cheerfully turn the other cheek and say, "God loves you and forgives you, and I love you and forgive you too."

Ignite in me, Lord, that divine anger that seeks relief for the unrelieved and justice for the victims of injustice. May the fire in my bones be the fire that burned in Jesus for the glory of your name and for the rescue of the people.

The Flame:

"In your anger do not sin": Do not let the sun go down while you are still angry.

Ephesians 4:26

FIRE IT UP!

Here are things you want me to be angry about, Lord:

_____

_____

_____

_____

_____

_____

_____

_____

My Passionate Prayer Time:

_____

_____

_____

_____

_____

_____

_____

_____

7

Burning to Thirst for You

I thirst for your truth, Lord.

    A thousand times a day,

        From a thousand sources,

            I get a thousand messages.

Radio, billboard, television, Internet, mailers, Facebook, Twitter, Instagram—all scream lies about life and truth and genuine meaning.

"Buy me and snatch success."

"Smell like me and you'll seduce your prey."

"Wear me and you'll rule Wall Street."

"Drink me and you'll have power."

"Follow me and you'll be the best in class, club, or company. In one hour."

PRESTO! Success! Power! Sex! Cash! Cool! Charisma! Cunning!

None of it speaks to LIFE'S BIGGEST THREE questions:

Why was I born?

What am I doing here?

Where am I going?

I thirst for your truth, O Lord. Only your truth embraces all three. I was created <u>by you</u> through the union of a man and a woman. I was born <u>for you</u> to fulfill your love and purpose on earth. I was born to be delivered <u>to you</u>, one day, for an eternal and heavenly homecoming.

Slap me each morning, Lord, and remind me that no coffee, commute, or companion takes the place of my morning time with you. Your word is cool and fresh in this hot and dry desert of earthly pain and regret. Only your word answers those Big Three questions.

And fill me up, allowing your rivers of living water to gush from me to revive others too parched to confess their thirst, or too proud to admit it. Amen.

The Flame:

I have hidden your word in my heart that I might not sin against you.

Psalm 119:11

"Whoever believes in me, as the Scripture has said, streams of living water will flow from within him."

John 7:38

FIRE IT UP!

This is how I thirst for God:

_____

_____

_____

_____

_____

_____

_____

_____

My Passionate Prayer Time:

_____

_____

_____

_____

_____

_____

_____

_____

8

Burning to Give Thanks

Lord, I know **an attitude of gratitude inspires altitude** for me and for others watching me. Remind me, Lord, that

- **A grateful mind** is a **great mind.**
- It is impossible to be thankful and worry at the same time.
- When I complain, I attract more of what I complain about, and when I give thanks, I get more of that for which I am thankful.

So, by your grace and power

- I will give thanks when I FEEL 105°-rays burning my cheeks, or when I feel 5°-sleet slapping my chin. I am grateful, Lord, that I can feel the outside world.
- I will give thanks that I SMELL the world. I will give thanks that my nostrils can breathe in the aroma of a blooming rose or the odors of a dead skunk.

- I will give thanks when I SEE the blue of the sky, the green of the grass, the lemon-orange burst of the morning sun, or the redness of my blood oozing from a wound.
- I will give thanks when I TASTE the cool, sweet, creamy layers of vanilla yogurt sliding on my tongue or the fiery seeds of a habañero pepper.
- I will give thanks when I HEAR the dulcet sounds of doves cooing to each other, or I hear the fierce sounds of screaming metal from the radio in the car next to me.

Remind me, Lord, of those Peace Corps days when I cared for lepers who could not feel, smell, see, taste, or hear. They ached for any sensory experience, pleasant or painful.

Remind me, Lord, to give thanks for the thousands of things I enjoy which money cannot buy. Remind me that if someone offered me a billion dollars for my left eye or right arm, I would not take it. I celebrate and give thanks for my priceless body.

I give thanks for my mother who never abandoned me. I give thanks for my wife who is always beside me. I give thanks for your truth written by your servant Paul that all things DO work together for good for those who love you and who are called according to your purpose (Romans 8:28).

You know, Lord, that I am not a masochist. I do not deliberately seek pain so that I can later see your purposes and feel your pleasure. I do know, however, that the pain is temporary, but your purposes are eternal and enduring.

And your pleasure of victory is certain.

And what a jolt of gratitude you gave me this morning, Lord. Thank you for the BANG, W-H-A-C-K on my forehead as the doctor and I puzzled over the report from the lab following my insurance exam. "Report Delayed," the lab said, "due to additional serum testing for malignancy, which is not an absolute test. Check with your doctor."

"I don't know what they're talking about," Dr. Morgan said. "Your PSA is good. So is your cholesterol, urine, BP, MRI, X-rays. What additional testing? What are they talking about?"

He called in his nurse. She couldn't figure it out. We called the lab. "Boilerplate language. We add those disclaimers to every report."

Dr. Morgan summed it up for me. "Look, the lab is saying to the insurance company, 'The reason we didn't get all the lab results in right away is because of additional testing. Takes a day or two. Standard disclosure. (And, oh, IF you're looking for traces of malignancy, or ANYTHING ELSE, serum tests are not a hundred percent accurate.) Again, it is a standard disclaimer basically saying that any scientific test is never going to be a hundred percent accurate.'"

Sheesh.

Why didn't they tell me that forty-eight hours ago when I first got the letter from the insurance company, rather than worrying about a mysterious and false malignancy growing in me?

"How long do I have to live?" That was the first question that came racing to my mind.

"Why, Lord, why do I have to wait and wonder?"

Oh, I hear you loud and clear, Lord. "I wanted you to be thankful for your billion-dollar healthy body. See how easily and how quickly it could be taken away?"

Perhaps that's what you were saying to me, Lord.

Got my life back.

Thank you, Lord.

The Flame:

Give thanks in all circumstances, for this is God's will for you in Christ Jesus.

1 Thessalonians 5:18

FIRE IT UP!

This is how I give thanks:

_____

_____

_____

_____

_____

_____

_____

_____

My Passionate Prayer Time:

_____

_____

_____

_____

_____

_____

_____

_____

9

Burning to Work

If you want to be a good witness for Jesus Christ on your job, then be the very best worker on your job.

—Robert L. Vernon,
Former Chief of Police,
Los Angeles Police Department

Genius is 1 percent inspiration and 99 percent perspiration.

—Thomas Edison

Lord, why is it that some people shun work once they get a job?

Is it "I'll grab all I can get" rather than "I'm grateful for all that I've been given"?

I don't understand.

Keep me burning, Lord, with a love of work.

Thank you, Lord, that at age five, you gave me work.

I delivered groceries in my little red cart, earning twelve cents an hour from grocer Charlie Coco.

Big job, big deal.

Just enough change to see two Roy Rogers movies, a Superman serial, and a Looney Tunes cartoon at the theater. And, with a nickel tip from Mrs. Rich (God, you had a sense of humor to give her that name), I bought a Bit-O-Honey candy bar and ate it all by myself.

Thank you that at age eleven I got another job delivering Sunday newspapers at five o'clock in the morning in February in Boston. I walked the streets, with my little nose as cold and hard as concrete, and clouds of frost gushing from my mouth.

Thank you that at age fifteen you gave me the work of cleaning muck raking those foot-high stacks of fertilizer dust that fell from the grinders. I arose early each Saturday to prepare more stacks for the crew on Monday to mix and grind more manure and pellets.

Some called it crap.

I called it gold. Working hard gave me money to help my welfare mom—and to buy a bike. That bike was used and scarred, but it rode like a flyer to me.

The work you provided rescued my mom and me from worrying and got us off welfare.

And in college I knew, "When the student is ready, the master will appear," and YOU did.

Tuition: a hundred dollars per semester. Remember, Lord? I didn't know there was a hundred dollars in the entire world, and you showed up with work. You gave me two jobs. During the week, Monday through Thursday, I assisted in the audio-visual library for the evening classes.

No calls? Slow night? Time for study. You provided for me even then.

And Friday through Saturday, I performed medic work at the local hospital. No calls? More slow nights? More time for study.

Some months I made two hundred dollars!

That money covered my tuition, books, food, and clothes and helped me to help Mom. Thank you, Lord.

Thank you, Lord, for work: that blazing fire of self-esteem that warms families and ignites progress, both public and personal. In my work (really your work), Lord, keep my focus intense and cheerful whether I'm cleaning toilets, fixing teeth, teaching a class, or trimming a hedgerow.

I will work with a passion for excellence knowing, by your grace and power, that all good work is honest and fulfilling and ultimately comes from your gracious hand.

Work is my daily devotion to you, Lord, and my daily gift to those dependent upon me to provide. Amen.

The Flame:

For even when we were with you, we gave you this rule: "The one who is unwilling to work shall not eat."

2 Thessalonians 3:10

FIRE IT UP!

This is how I work:

_____

_____

_____

_____

_____

_____

_____

_____

My Passionate Prayer Time:

_____

_____

_____

_____

_____

_____

_____

_____

_____

10

Burning for Eternity with You

Lord, you know I love my wife,
> my children,
>> the people in my church,
>>> my clients,
>>>> my fellow Americans.

I cherish the fellowship of friends, delight in helping clients, and exalt at the opportunities to grow and serve you in the body of Christ. I enjoy the ecstasy of victory and the agony of defeat. (OK, I don't "enjoy" the agony, but I know it's necessary for growth.)

I love being alive, but I want to be with you, Lord. I want to see you face to face.

Is that OK?

After all, what is this life all about?

After shopping at the store, studying at school, playing at the park, or working at the factory or office, we want to go home.

I want to go home. I want to be with you, the One who knew me when I was in the womb, who brought me to life, and who nourished and nurtured me all these years. I want to be with my Father, the source of unconditional love. Make me ready to see you, Lord. Prepare a place for me where you are, so I can be there too.

The Flame:

For to me, to live is Christ and to die is gain. If I am to go on living in the body, this will mean fruitful labor for me. Yet what shall I choose? I do not know! I am torn between the two: I desire to depart and be with Christ, which is better by far.

Philippians 1:21–23

FIRE IT UP!

Here's how I'm burning to be with you:

_____

_____

_____

_____

_____

_____

_____

_____

My Passionate Prayer Time:

_____

_____

_____

_____

_____

_____

_____

_____

11

Burning for Your Power

Lord, why is it that some people are intrigued and fascinated by brutality and wickedness? It seems like they want to wield power that is out of control, like watching a horror movie, maybe?

Thank you, Lord, that you've shown me by your word and by the life of Jesus that power means service to all and strength under control. It means humility and charity. It's like the picture of Hulk Hogan holding an egg in his hand while he flexes his muscles. The egg does not shatter because he keeps his strength under control.

Power, <u>Jesus style,</u> is in the word meekness, isn't it? Jesus taught that power awaits those who are meek and great rewards for those who are poor in spirit. The meek have the power and the control, and they channel it toward positive ends by offering service.

Meekness is what the world needs most. Right, Lord?

When I taught in the university, Lord, I explored the writings of Niccolo Machiavelli, who believed exploitation of power to be a virtue and deception the best possible means to gaining supreme advantage. Sounds like your enemy, Satan, the father of lies and the author of all power grabbing.

Lord, you are the ultimate contrast to those Machiavellian-like attitudes and principles that shatter human relationships. You desire truth in the innermost parts of me, Lord, that I should not seek to glory in myself but exalt you and your righteous ways in all I do. I desire that too. Amen.

The Flame:

Do nothing out of selfish ambition or vain conceit. Rather, in humility value others above yourselves, not looking to your own interests but each of you to the interests of others. In your relationships with one another, have the same mindset as Christ Jesus: Who, being in very nature God, did not consider equality with God something to be used to his own advantage; rather, he made himself nothing by taking the very nature of a servant, being made in human likeness.

Philippians 2:3–7

FIRE IT UP!

Here's how I am burning for your power and using it to serve others:

_____

_____

_____

_____

_____

_____

_____

My Passionate Prayer Time:

_____

_____

_____

_____

_____

_____

_____

_____

12

Burning to Give and Give and Give

Lord, I fight the fear of "not enough."

After fifty years of experiencing your faithfulness, I still flirt with thoughts like, "Will there be enough left for me?" It doesn't matter if the dollar amount is $2, $22,000, or somewhere in between. I still fight my pen when it wants to add more zeroes to those sums on my checks.

Help me, Lord, to give hilariously. Remind me that GIVING IS YOUR GIFT to me.

I know it was no accident, Lord, that day when someone left that *Guidepost* magazine lying flat on the library table. I slid it aside to open the *Wall Street Journal*, but the *Guidepost* title grabbed me. "Gusher on God's Ground: To Give or Not to Give?" Hardly a recent story, it told of a tiny West Texas church decades ago that discovered on their crabgrass parking lot a mini Spindle Top, a nice, messy, spouting gusher.

A petroleum engineer said they'd receive $3,500 a month in royalties.

For a church on a $790-a-month budget that spelled instant wealth.

Then came the Wednesday night meeting of the deacons, and they were preparing for Sunday's service. A young guy quipped, "We can leave the tithes and offering part of the service out. We don't need offerings anymore. We're going to be receiving about $3,500 a month coming in from them royalties."

Back then, that was lots of money and would be today too!

But Brother Ledbetter, the oldest and wisest among them, stood and declared: "No, we'll still have the offering this Sunday and every Sunday. We'll still ask people to give for the widows, the orphans, the support of the church, for missions, for education, for the preacher, for benevolence. We'll still challenge them to give like we always do. We'll still have the offering: we give because we need to give. If we didn't give, we would dry up and die."

Was it by accident or angels that I read that article?

Remind me, Lord, that if I—if we—did not give, we would dry up and die. Giving-receiving, giving-receiving, giving-receiving. Your biology laws roar with that lesson.

Humans give CO_2 when we exhale. Plants receive the CO_2 for life.

Plants give O_2 when they exhale. Humans receive the O_2 for life.

The cycle of robust life.

Give or die.

Jesus himself said, "It is more blessed to give than to receive."

Acts 20:35

And the serendipity (thank you, Lord) is realizing that the more I give, the more I receive. Much more.

I stretch to give a dollar, and I get back $20.

I stretch to give $20, and I get back $250.

I stretch to give $1,500, and I get back $6,200.

Sometimes, the shower of money comes as an unexpected bonus, a repayment of a loan, or a letter from the Internal Revenue Service notifying me of a refund I was not expecting.

Lord, I want to give excessively and not hold on so tightly that the love of money strangles my life.

Thank you, Lord, for reminding me about the primitive hunters in Africa who trap monkeys. A crate with a small neck holds a banana at the bottom of the crate. The neck is wide enough to slide a hand in if the hand is open, fingers extended. The monkey slides his hand in, grabs the banana. Trying to retrieve the banana, the monkey now has a closed fist. Closed fists won't fit through the small opening of the crate. The monkey's too dumb to realize he's got to LET GO, so he can slide his hand out.

So the monkey with a closed fist is pulling and tugging and pulling and tugging. He's trapped by the crate because of his greed. He's stuck until a hunter arrives and whacks him over the head and then roasts him for dinner.

Thank you for your patience as you teach me the law of letting go: that the looser my grip on material things, the more tightly you wrap your arms of provision around my life. Everything is opposite with you, Lord.

Thank you, Lord, that your law of giving is the opposite of the law of gravity. Gravity pushes us down, giving pulls us up. As I relax my grip on material things, you shower me with unbelievable blessings.

Upside-down gravity applies to more than just money, doesn't it?

Your principle is: "Whatever you need, GIVE it to another."

Feeling lonely and friendless? Befriend and help another—pulling them up pulls you up. Feeling depressed and discouraged? Encourage another—pulling them up pulls you up. Feeling broke and scared? Give money to another—pulling them up pulls you up.

Thank you, Lord, for turning the law of gravity upside down. Or maybe right side up. Instead of feeling exhausted by giving, giving, giving, we feel elevated and energetic.

And by your grace and power, Lord, I will be a go-*giver*, not a go-*getter*.

And thank you for etching your law of giving <u>in writing</u>:

"Will a mere mortal rob God? Yet you rob me.
But you ask, 'How are we robbing you?' In tithes

and offerings. You are under a curse—your whole nation—because you are robbing me. Bring the whole tithe into the storehouse, that there may be food in my house. 'Test me in this,' says the LORD Almighty, 'and see if I will not throw open the floodgates of heaven and pour out so much bless-ing that you will not have enough room to share it. I will prevent pests from devouring your crops, and the vines in your fields will not drop their fruit before it is ripe,' says the LORD Almighty."

Malachi 3:8–11

The Flame:

Each of you should give what you have decided in your heart to give, not reluctantly or under compulsion, for God loves a cheerful giver.

2 Corinthians 9:7

FIRE IT UP!

This is how I give to you:

_____

_____

_____

_____

_____

_____

_____

_____

My Passionate Prayer Time:

_____

_____

_____

_____

_____

_____

_____

_____

13

Burning to Pray

Lord, things probably look to this lunch bunch at Olive Garden like I'm talking to thin air. Maybe they think I'm mouthing mantras to Vishnu or to the tooth fairy or to the Easter bunny.

Maybe they think I'm drunk and mumbling. They don't know I'm praying to you.

What they think really doesn't matter to me. I'm glad for the power and pleasure of prayer. You said, "I want all men everywhere to be in prayer." You didn't say, ". . . unless you're out in public." You didn't say, ". . . unless other people are watching." You didn't say, ". . . unless you're in a bad mood."

Lord, it's kind of like a guy loving his wife, isn't it? You say anywhere, anytime: "I love you." It comes naturally, supernaturally, really because that kind of love is a miracle just like prayer.

Isn't that what prayer is, Lord? I say, "I love you, I trust you, I need you, and I appreciate you." It comes from you. I'm thrilled to feel your presence and embrace your direction anytime I bow to you.

That reminds me of the day, Lord, when I interviewed former Governor Mike Huckabee. I asked him, "Governor, you're obviously a Christian and pray a lot. Does God speak to you audibly when you pray?"

"No," he said. "It's stronger than that!"

Wonderful reply!

And thank you, Lord, for the powerful lesson you taught me when Nick, years ago, showed me that—indeed—God's men and women pray everywhere.

We were in the rotunda of the Pennsylvania state capitol in Harrisburg headed upstairs. Fifty of us had signed a petition, (remember that, Lord?), pressing for a bill to stop child trafficking, and we were now about to appear before the Senate committee to demand action.

Nick said, "Let's pray before we go upstairs."

"Now?" I questioned. "Right here in the lobby?"

Nick directed all of us in the group to make a circle around the state symbol that had been colorfully emblazoned on the gleaming marble floor. We prayed and sang. FedEx couriers, secretaries, and janitors stopped on the outside of our circle and watched and listened intently. Dozens of lawyers draped in black suits, silver threads running along the rich cloth with cufflinks gleaming, careened around the circle, racing for the elevators.

We got the power.

You got the glory.

We testified.

You won.

I'm burning to pray, Lord, because it helps me fight my arrogance in thinking I can do it all myself.

When I pray, I am not blinded by flashes of panic. When I pray, I see the sunlight of solutions. I rise from prayer and know you are bigger than my problems.

I am burning to pray, Lord, because each time I pray, I see that you have given me a mind to think, a voice to speak, hands to write, and a body to move forward in embracing solutions and implementing strategies to help myself and to help others.

I am burning to pray, Lord, because when I pray, I am reminded of what you told Gideon: "Look and see the army of angels I have prepared to protect you."

PS. Did you see that, Lord? This guy came up to me at my booth just now, while I was finishing my dinner and said: "Sir, thank you very much. More of us need to be praying all of the time don't we? I believe I'll start doing it myself." Amen.

The Flame:

In your light we see light.

Psalm 36:9

May my prayer be set before you like incense; may the lifting up of my hands be like the evening sacrifice.

Psalm 141:2

Ask and it will be given to you; seek and you will find; knock and the door will be opened to you. For everyone who asks receives; he who seeks finds; and to him who knocks, the door will be opened.

Matthew 7:7–8

If you believe, you will receive whatever you ask for in prayer.

Matthew 21:22

Do not be anxious about anything, but in every situation, by prayer and petition, with thanksgiving, present your requests to God.

Philippians 4:6

FIRE IT UP!

This is how I pray:

_____

_____

_____

_____

_____

_____

_____

_____

_____

My Passionate Prayer Time:

_____

_____

_____

_____

_____

_____

_____

_____

_____

14

Burning to be a Miracle

Lord, I want my life to be a miracle of your powerful service. Famed runner Eric Liddell said in *Chariots of Fire*: "So where does the power come from? It comes from within, where Christ is, ruling in our hearts."

You provide the opportunities, Lord, and wherever you send me, you get the credit.

You know the needs. You send the servant. That's the way it works, right?

You did it with Philip and the Ethiopian official.

Man with need, this Ethiopian rattling along in a chariot. He's reading Isaiah.

And he's confused. You prepared the man with the need, and then you prepared a man to fill the need, Philip. Philip's open to your leading, so the Holy Spirit sends him to ride alongside the Ethiopian. And the rest is history:

The Spirit told Philip, "Go to that chariot and stay near it."

Then Philip ran up to the chariot and heard the man reading Isaiah the prophet. "Do you understand what you are reading?" Philip asked.

"How can I," he said, "unless someone explains it to me?" So he invited Philip to come up and sit with him.

This is the passage of Scripture the eunuch was reading:

"He was led like a sheep to the slaughter, and as a lamb before its shearer is silent, so he did not open his mouth.

"In his humiliation he was deprived of justice. Who can speak of his descendants? For his life was taken from the earth."

The eunuch asked Philip, "Tell me, please, who is the prophet talking about, himself or someone else?"

Then Philip began with that very passage of Scripture and told him the good news about Jesus.

As they traveled along the road, they came to some water and the eunuch said, "Look, here is water. What can stand in the way of my being baptized?"

And he gave orders to stop the chariot. Then both Philip and the eunuch went down into the water and Philip baptized him.

When they came up out of the water, the Spirit of the Lord suddenly took Philip away, and the eunuch did not see him again, but went on his way rejoicing.

Acts 8:29–39

Ditto with Cornelius and Peter. Man with need on a porch. Cornelius, a Roman centurion, looking for direction. He's praying. He wants help.

You prepared the man with the need, and you prepared the man to fill the need, Peter. Fighting his prejudices against Gentiles, Peter finds himself on the porch with Cornelius.

And the rest is history:

At Caesarea there was a man named Cornelius, a centurion in what was known as the Italian Regiment.

He and all his family were devout and God-fearing; he gave generously to those in need and prayed to God regularly.

One day at about three in the afternoon he had a vision. He distinctly saw an angel of God, who came to him and said, "Cornelius!"

Cornelius stared at him in fear. "What is it, Lord?" he asked.

The angel answered, "Your prayers and gifts to the poor have come up as a memorial offering before God.

"Now send men to Joppa to bring back a man named Simon who is called Peter.

"He is staying with Simon the tanner, whose house is by the sea."

Acts 10:1–6

So Simon met Peter, and

Then Peter said, "Can anyone keep these people from being baptized with water? [Cornelius and his household]. They have received the Holy Spirit just as we have."

So he ordered that they be baptized in the name of Jesus Christ. Then they asked Peter to stay with them for a few days.

Acts 10:47–48

Both Philip and Peter had hearts for service: "Lord, here I am, send me."

Burning to be a miracle for you.

Lord, I want to be that same kind of miracle of your service. After all, I AM a miracle. My conception was a miracle.

My new birth, surrendering to Jesus and being born again, was a miracle. My first breath was a miracle. Your breath of new life at my salvation was a miracle.

No computer could ever replace my brain. "The brain's a miracle," Dr. Ben Carson, the esteemed pediatric neurosurgeon and hero of the movie *Gifted Hands*, announced to his skeptical colleagues at Johns Hopkins. Sorting, sifting, solving, remembering, projecting, imaging, there's nothing like it. It's a miracle. No man-made lenses could ever replace my eyes; they are miracles. My pupils know how and when to adjust to light and darkness—a miracle. My pupils capture, in a glance, a wide football field yet can bring into immediate focus the tiny point of a toothpick.

No amps could ever replace my ears. They can capture the coo of a dove in one ear and the blare of a siren in the other ear—a miracle. No gadgets could ever replace my arms and fingers. They're tender enough to feel the brush of a blanket, yet tough enough to seize a sledgehammer—a miracle.

I am a miracle. Thank you, Lord, and I want my life to be a miracle of your service. Amen.

The Flame:

In the same way, let your light shine before others, that they may see your good deeds and glorify your Father in heaven.

Matthew 5:16

I praise you because I am fearfully and wonderfully made; your works are wonderful, I know that full well.

Psalm 139:14

FIRE IT UP!

Here's how I will make my life a miracle of your service, Lord:

_____

_____

_____

_____

_____

_____

_____

_____

My Passionate Prayer Time:

_____

_____

_____

_____

_____

_____

_____

_____

_____

15

Burning to Rid the World of "Religion"

What's this "Christianity" stuff, God? Bible college, seminaries, even church services—places where they should know

- "Why Christianity is the only true religion."
- "He was converted to Christianity while he was in the military."
- "The earthly and material benefits of Christianity."
- And on and on.

For openers, "Christianity" is not in the Bible. When I responded to the invitation decades ago, Lord, I surrendered to YOU; I fell in love with you and came under the conviction of your Holy Spirit. I fell in love with a Savior, not a system. I embraced a relationship with one who loves me, not a religion that limits me. I surrendered to one who loves me unconditionally. I didn't surrender to arbitrary rules or traditions that torment and confuse.

God, how did they—how did we—miss it when your word flashes the truth with neon brightness?

- <u>Christ</u> is our hope. Not a religion entangled with tradition and politics.
- <u>Christ</u> has set us free. Not religious rules. A person went to the cross and out of the tomb. Not a religion.
- "I am the resurrection and the life." Not Christianity. Christianity never raised anyone and never will.

So basic.

Religion is fearing, finding, hoping to please a distant, unknowable God. Hindus chanting in their temple. Muslims bowing in their mosques. Pagans cutting their bodies. But me? Christ, your Son, is the living, powerful God, passionately alive in me, releasing his life of love through me to love others by his Spirit.

For to me, to live is Christ and to die is gain.

Philippians 1:21

So I want to burn for Jesus, Lord, not for religion because in the alphabet of my heart Jesus is—

A the Apple of my eye, the angel of light, and my powerful Advocate

B the Beauty of lilies

C the Christ—the one all creation was awaiting; my Counselor

D the Divine healer

E the Eternal light of the ages

F the Friend of sinners; the first fruits of all creation

G God incarnate; a Guide for me

H the Holy of holies; the hope of the world; the Helper of all

I Incarnation of all that's pure and lovely

J Jesus, of course, the sweetest name on earth

K King of kings

L Lord of lords

M the Messiah and my mentor and Master

N Neil's reason to live and die

O the Object of everyone's affection and longing

P patient, believing in me, disciplining me, rescuing me, and rewarding; Prince of peace

Q the quiet assurance of my soul

R the Redeemer and my Rock

S Savior of all the world

T the Triumphant leader of angels when he returns to claim his own

U the Undisputed Creator and sustainer of life

V Victory for the faithful

W the Wonder of it all; your answer to Why was I born? Why am I here?

X the seer of all things like an X-ray into my soul and spirit and my thoughts

Y Your friend and Savior, comforter, and deliverer

Z the last letter—the Omega. He is alpha and omega; the beginning and the end

That's why I burn for Jesus and not religion (Philippians 1:21).

So when they tell me to keep religion out of business, politics, government, and schools, I'll say, "Yes, yes, yes," but I will not—I cannot—keep Christ out of business, politics, government, and schools. Like Luther said: "Here I stand. I can do no other, God help me."

I know not what course others may take, but I follow a Redeemer, not a religion.

> "Do this and live, religion demands,
> But gives me neither feet nor hands.
> A better word, Jesus Christ, does bring.
> He gives me power and gives me wings."

We are therefore Christ's ambassadors, as though God were making his appeal through us. We implore you on Christ's behalf: Be reconciled to God.

2 Corinthians 5:20

The Flame:

Simon Peter answered him, "Lord, to whom shall we go? You have the words of eternal life. We believe and know that you are the Holy One of God."

John 6:68

Jesus answered, "If I want him to remain alive until I return, what is that to you? You must follow me."

John 21:22

FIRE IT UP!

This is how I rid the world of religion and replace it with Christ:

_____

_____

_____

_____

_____

_____

_____

_____

My Passionate Prayer Time:

_____

_____

_____

_____

_____

_____

_____

_____

16

Burning for Purpose

Lord, etch on the front lobe of my brain the message that's on the fridge magnet: "If money were no object, what would I do with my life?"

And help me to refine that message by adding to it: "If a person doesn't have something worth dying for, he has nothing worth living for."

When I die, Lord, and they form a ring around that black hole, I want the eulogy to focus on you and not on me. I want them to say, "Here was a man who died saying, 'Make my life a miracle of your service, Lord.' This man was a channel of God's unconditional love, of 24/7 service to people, all people. Because of Jesus."

For all people are made in your image, Lord.

I want to be that man D. L. Moody talked about when he said, "The world has yet to see what God will do with a man fully consecrated to Him."

The average life span of a mayfly is a brief twenty-four hours. This tiny winged insect is born, reaches maturity, mates, and dies in the span of just one of our normal days. One twenty-four hour day. One of our normal days.

It seems foolish to us for the mayfly to waste even one moment in light of such a short life span!

From Your perspective of eternity, God, billions of years, our life span appears to be one twenty-four-hour day. It doesn't make sense to waste even one minute of it, when we can enjoy Your power, God, that you entrusted to us for every moment of our lives. Amen.

The Flame:

Why, you do not even know what will happen tomorrow. What is your life? You are a mist that appears for a little while and then vanishes.

James 4:14

Then he said to them, "Watch out! Be on your guard against all kinds of greed; life does not consist in an abundance of possessions."

Luke 12:15

FIRE IT UP!

This is how I burn for purpose:

_____

_____

_____

_____

_____

_____

_____

_____

My Passionate Prayer Time:

_____

_____

_____

_____

_____

_____

_____

_____

Burning for Family

17

Burning to Honor my Wife

Lord, shut my mouth when I'm tempted to join the banter of buffoons who demean their wives publicly—and women in general.

- Locker room
- Subway
- Bowling alley
- Office deli
- Church lobby
- Airport lounge—wherever.

"The only time my wife's mouth is shut is when she stuffs it with food."

"My wife said to me this morning, 'Honey, we can't be out of money. There are still checks in my checkbook.'"

"All the time. ALL THE TIME she's late. Bet she'll be late for her own funeral."

And this classic: "'But, officer,' my wife pleaded with the mad cop writing a ticket, 'they had no right to complain. If they didn't like the way I was driving, they should have gotten off the sidewalk.'"

Remind me, Lord, that when she hears these barbs, she's laughing on the outside (to join the fun), but she's crying on the inside.

Lord, rip me from the company of

- Archie Bunker,
- Cartoon Simpson , or
- Any other rude dude who cuts his queen with words.

I honor women, and I honor my wife, Lord.

And, Lord, thank you for all the women you have raised who personify breath-grasping adventures in unconditional love and uncommon courage:

- Esther,
- Mary, the mother of Jesus,
- Harriet Tubman,
- Mother Teresa,
- Amy Carmichael,
- Clara Barton,
- Rosa Parks,
- Elisabeth Elliot,
- Dr. Helen Brooke Tausig,
- My mother who sang and danced before her ten- and thirteen-year-old sons who forgot they were cold and hungry,

- My wife, who has poured her life into rescuing millions of children who cannot speak for themselves, and
- All <u>Mothers</u> everywhere.

Lord, I thank you for woman, and I honor her.

I will let no pornographer exploit her, no man abuse her, no company demean her, no government patronize her, and no child disrespect her.

Use me to blast the politically correct image of today's woman who allegedly

- punches like Tyson,
- sweats like the Hulk,
- swears like a bouncer, and
- flirts like Lady Gaga.

And, thank you, Lord, that I have opportunities each and every day to honor every woman in my life, especially my wife, recognizing that woman is a queen of comfort, a cocoon of calm, the cradle of birth and regeneration, and the civilizing force in every man's life.

Lord, she is your finest creation, the epitome of Jesus's words: ". . . the meek shall inherit the earth."

She radiates compassion with her nurturing nature, displays wisdom with her unique intuition, and magnifies meekness in her balance of *strength* under *control*, that synergy you planted in her left-brain and right-brain spheres.

Lord, I thank you for my wife; I honor her.

I am burning to unpack her treasures.

Remind me, Lord, that I married a treasure of emotions. When I married my wife, I married into a history of

- Feelings
- Troubles
- Memories
- Prejudices
- Strengths
- Weaknesses
- Victories
- Habits.

And only in time will I discover how priceless the treasure is, Lord.

There could be some soiled rugs hidden at the bottom of her treasure chest, as well as an opal heirloom from Grandmother.

There could be my wife's tear-stained diary, as well as an oilskin family Bible with a hundred years of genealogy in it.

There could be receipts from a psychiatric clinic, or there could be a college yearbook full of cheerleading awards.

Empower me with a healthy curiosity to unpack her treasure WITH RESPECT throughout all our married life. Empower me to communicate to her, Lord, that she can unpack everything from her treasure chest and tell me all. She can show it all to me, without fear of shame or surprise.

Hey, I've got my own history, warts and all.

- Memories
- Stories
- Mistakes

- Prejudices
- Failures

She's not the only one in our marriage who has hit bottom at times.

Empower me, with my wife, to radiate your Spirit of reciprocity and openness, allowing her to KNOW that I want to listen and to L-O-O-K at her while I am listening.

- I close Facebook.
- I shut off the computer.
- I stuff the cell phone under the pillow.
- I toss the paper to the floor, and I look and I listen.

I will not say, "That was stupid."

I will not say, "Well, that is easy to fix."

I will not say, "Let me tell you what happened to me."

I will not say, "I can't believe that you did that. Why didn't you tell me that before we were married?"

I celebrate the fact that I married a treasure, mine to enjoy and explore for fifty years of marriage or better. Amen.

The Flame:

Husbands, in the same way be considerate as you live with your wives, and treat them with respect as the weaker partner and as heirs with you of the gracious gift of life, so that nothing will hinder your prayers.

1 Peter 3:7

FIRE IT UP!

This is how I honor my wife:

_____

_____

_____

_____

_____

_____

_____

_____

My Passionate Prayer Time:

_____

_____

_____

_____

_____

_____

_____

_____

18

Burning for Intimacy

The bonfire is marriage.

Lord, you are a

- Smart Savior,
- Practical Father,
- Healthy Guide, and
- Romantic Ruler.

You planted testosterone in man to seek ultimate fulfillment in woman. You delight in man's attraction to woman. You love the libido you gave man. You love the intimacy dwelling in a woman and so appealing to a man.

She is naturally alluring, naturally magnetic. Thank you.

Man, the hunter. Woman, the hunted. (Until she catches him!)

And what a picture: *The two shall become one.*

That is why a man leaves his father and mother and is united to his wife, and they become one flesh.

Genesis 2:24

Where else is that dramatized more passionately than in the marriage act? One man + one woman = one life of intimate ecstasy in the faithful bond of marriage.

<u>That's what I call one heaven of a party!</u>

Help me in that partying time to seek her pleasure first. You know, Lord, in my manliness, I'm hot and ready. I want to release. Remind me, Lord, to ask, "What's your pleasure? How can I help you, the bride of my life, to enjoy the intensity of this moment?"

Remind me, Lord, that, well, she and I are different.

Hallelujah. That's your creative genius!

I'm quick and hot; she's slow and warm. For me, sex IS the love.

For her, feeling loved, important, and secure provides a melodic prelude to intimacy and romance.

You remind me of that truth, Lord, every time I am counseling with a couple struggling with intimacy.

She says: "I have to feel secure and settled before our passionate embrace." He says: "Hey, let's do the passion. THAT will make you feel secure and settled."

Remind me, Lord, with the beautiful bride you've given me, to love her s-l-o-w-l-y.

Lord, you have given me my libido that can be enjoyed for lust or for love. Lead me to channel it for love with my lifetime lover.

And one more thing, gracious Lord: Prompt me to pray for the millions of men who are missing it. They think a stud is a guy who sleeps with hundreds. But all they get are STDs and a lifetime of sorrow.

For them and the hundreds they've seduced.

Help them to see that super sex requires godly strength, self-control, gentle patience, manly discipline, and common sense.

Big lover gives his life <u>first</u>. In marriage: life first, body second. A super-stud.

Thank you, Lord, for intimacy with my lifetime spiritual partner, bonded together in the fire of wedding vows. Amen.

The Flame:

The husband should fulfill his marital duty to his wife, and likewise the wife to her husband. The wife does not have authority over her own body but yields it to her husband. In the same way, the husband does not have authority over his own body but yields it to his wife.

1 Corinthians 7:3–4

FIRE IT UP!

This is how I burn for intimacy with my marriage mate:

_____

_____

_____

_____

_____

_____

_____

_____

My Passionate Prayer Time:

_____

_____

_____

_____

_____

_____

_____

_____

19

Burning to "Man up" for Wife and Family

Well, Lord, did you notice? Science proved it. Apparently, that settles it.

Maybe.

It seems like every time that science makes a new discovery, the science world forgets to acknowledge that YOU are the originator of it all. All scientific principles, newly discovered, are embedded eternally in your Word.

You saw, Lord, where the scientists took a group of infants: baby boys in one room, baby girls in another. Sure enough, the boys were aggressive, took risks, and clamored for leadership. The girls were relational, team oriented, and very nurturing with each other.

How about that?

Looks like it's not culture or training or sexism or desire for power or anything else. It's just man's nature to lead, and woman's nature to nurture. Thank you, Creator God.

Yes, I know through training they can—and should—reciprocate, but right now we are talking about what is congenital, natural, genetic, and biological.

Lord, you made us men with a burning to explore and a burning to lead.

At times we move dangerously because we like to find the unknown. And because we have a passion for excellence, we like to push the limits.

Jesus said: "Risk your life and get more than you ever dreamed of. Play it safe, and end up holding the bag" (Luke 19:26, *The Message*).

We know that if we surrender to the side of security

- great inventions would never have erupted
- great medical breakthroughs would never have happened
- great movements of missions and evangelism never would have been realized via the Hudson Taylors, Dwight Moodys, and Billy Grahams of the world.

We find out quickly—thank you, Lord—that it's right and good that we men do the things that we were made for—to plow ahead, to lead with courage, to protect with resolve. That's what it's like to be a man. We accept the challenge of leadership.

Dare, risk, explore, challenge, protect. That's us men.

Thank you, Lord. And because of that leadership drive you gave me and other men, I commit myself to the words of that majestic song "Lead Me" composed by my friends Matthew Hammitt, Jason Ingram, and Christopher James Rohman.

Lead Me*

In picture frames I see my beautiful wife
Always smiling
But on the inside, I can hear her saying . . .

"Lead me with strong hands
Stand up when I can't
Don't leave me hungry for love
Chasing dreams; what about us?

"Show me you're willing to fight
That I'm still the love of your life
I know we call this our home
But I still feel alone."

I see my kids' faces, look in their innocent eyes
They're just children from the outside
I'm working hard, I tell myself they'll be fine
They're independent
But on the inside, I can hear them saying,

"Lead me with strong hands
So Father, give me the strength
To be everything I'm called to be
Oh, Father, show me the way
To lead them
Won't You lead me?"

* Used with gratitude and by permission, Capitol CMG Publishing, Brentwood, TN.

The Flame:

Anyone who does not provide for their relatives, and especially for his own household, has denied the faith and is worse than an unbeliever.

1 Timothy 5:8

Husbands, love your wives, just as Christ loved the church and gave himself up for her to make her holy, cleansing her by the washing with water through the word, and to present her to himself as a radiant church, without stain or wrinkle or any other blemish, but holy and blameless.

Ephesians 5:25–27

FIRE IT UP!

This is how I "man up"; this is how I lead:

_____

_____

_____

_____

_____

_____

_____

_____

My Passionate Prayer Time:

_____

_____

_____

_____

_____

_____

_____

_____

20

Burning to Submit

Submit to one another, you said, Lord.

One's the head, the other's the heart. What a team. Got to have both. Submission showcases the principle: **you can either be right, or you can be happy**. Happy husbands and happy wives submit to each other. And they grow in their happiness.

Yes, I know, in the nature of human relations, any team's got to have someone who makes the final decision. In family and in spiritual matters, that's the man, the husband, the father.

The guy. He's the one that's got the burden of responsibility, making ultimate decisions, fulfilling plans that impact the whole family.

Wow! What a responsibility. I know it. I feel it. And, at times, I fear it.

She says all that she wants to say, and he says all that he wants to say. They report their feelings accurately, directly, lovingly. Then at the end of the day, somebody's got to decide.

In the meantime, they submit to each other.

"Wait," I hear offstage. "You said in an earlier *Fire* about *burning to lead*. These don't seem to go together. How can you be burning to lead and burning to submit?"

They DO go together. **Before someone becomes a good leader, he learns to be a good follower.** He learns to submit. He learns to surround himself with people who are smarter than he is. He learns to ask, sift, and pray. Burning to submit and burning to lead. They go together. Lord, teach me to ever follow **your** gracious lead in submitting to the will of my Father, so that I can be a better leader. Amen.

The Flame:

Wives, submit yourselves to your own husbands as you do to the Lord. For the husband is the head of the wife as Christ is the head of the church, his body, of which he is the Savior. Now as the church submits to Christ, so also wives should submit to their husbands in everything.

Ephesians 5:22–24

FIRE IT UP!

Here's how I submit:

_____

_____

_____

_____

_____

_____

_____

_____

My Passionate Prayer Time:

_____

_____

_____

_____

_____

_____

_____

_____

21

Burning to Build a Stool

Lord, I don't like these business trips, but by your grace and power, I'm going to build a stool, a three-legged stool, right here in my hotel room.

Leg 1. I rip the TV cord from the wall, so I will not collapse under the spell of the one-eyed Satan who wants me to watch adult films or shock reality shows or give-me-more greed games.

Leg 2. I lay my Bible on my pillow and open it to Psalm 23, a reminder of my Source, my comfort, and my accountability.

Leg 3. I lift the phone to call my wife.

Bang, bang, bang

- No TV
- Open Bible
- Love talk with my wife

And I surround it all with prayer. Now, I'm protected in this room, whether it's a one-night stay or a one-month stay.

Lord, give me opportunity to help other men to build this three-legged stool in their hotel rooms. I know there are lives (and so do you, Lord) that have been ravaged by greed, lust, envy, or hate swirling within the cage of a hotel room that has become a cabaret of demonic activity.

I am protected by you.

Just look at the Yellow Pages, Lord. Under *Escort*: "Call us now and we will send a lady to your room." And then there's the sleazy billboard: "What happens in Vegas stays in Vegas." (What a crock that is.)

The picture of the *Escort* in the Yellow Pages with her bikini bra about to bust and in a short miniskirt above fish-net hose kind of gives you the impression that she is NOT coming to your room to play chess.

I need to see, Lord, and help other men to see, that this hotel time is a time to pray, think, write. Then go downstairs and hit the weights and treadmill. Sexual temptation is energy, which can be poured into building mind and muscle and soul.

Here I go.

Now I'm back. I did it: I hit the exercise room, listened to a motivational tape, and directed my energy to Pure, Positive, and Productive outlets. Then I returned to this room, called my wife, and read your Word. I am ready for happy and holy rest. And I am ready for a pure and positive day tomorrow. Amen.

The Flame:

Be alert and of sober mind. Your enemy the devil prowls around like a roaring lion looking for someone to devour.

1 Peter 5:8

No temptation has overtaken you except what is common to mankind. And God is faithful; he will not let you be tempted beyond what you can bear. But when you are tempted, he will also provide a way out so that you can endure it.

1 Corinthians 10:13

FIRE IT UP!

Here's how I help other men to build a three-legged stool:

_____

_____

_____

_____

_____

_____

_____

My Passionate Prayer Time:

_____

_____

_____

_____

_____

_____

_____

_____

22

Burning to Promise

I'm in, Lord.

All in.

I am a Promise Keeper.

Promise 1: I promise to honor Jesus Christ through worship, prayer, and obedience to His Word in the power of the Holy Spirit.

The Flame:

I have been crucified with Christ and I no longer live, but Christ lives in me. The life I now live in the body, I live by faith in the Son of God, who loved me and gave himself for me.

Galatians 2:20

Promise 2: I promise to pursue authentic and committed relationships with other men, knowing that I need brothers to help me keep my promises and my brothers need me for mutual support.

The Flame:

A friend loves at all times, and a brother is born for a time of adversity.

Proverbs 17:17

As iron sharpens iron, so one person sharpens another.

Proverbs 27:17

Promise 3: I promise to practice spiritual, moral, ethical, and sexual purity.

The Flame:

Dear friends, I urge you, as foreigners and exiles, to abstain from sinful desires, which wage war against your soul. Live such good lives among the pagans that, though they accuse you of doing wrong, they may see your good deeds and glorify God on the day he visits us.

1 Peter 2:11–12

Promise 4: I promise to build a strong marriage and a strong family through love, protection, and biblical values and to help other men do the same.

The Flame:

Impress them on your children. Talk about them when you sit at home and when you walk along the road, when you lie down and when you get up.

Deuteronomy 6:7

In this same way, husbands ought to love their wives as their own bodies. He who loves his wife loves himself.

Ephesians 5:28

Promise 5: I promise to support the mission of my church by honoring and praying for my pastor and fellow members and by actively giving my time and resources.

The Flame:

I rejoiced greatly in the Lord that at last you renewed your concern for me. Indeed, you were concerned, but you had no opportunity to show it. I am not saying this because I am in need, for I have learned to be content whatever the

*circumstances. I know what it is to be in need,
and I know what it is to have plenty. I have
learned the secret of being content in any and
every situation, whether well fed or hungry,
whether living in plenty or in want. I can do all
this through him who gives me strength. Yet it was
good of you to share in my troubles. Moreover, as
you Philippians know, in the early days of your
acquaintance with the gospel, when I set out
from Macedonia, not one church shared with me
in the matter of giving and receiving, except you
only; for even when I was in Thessalonica, you
sent me aid more than once when I was in need.
Not that I desire your gifts; what I desire is that
more be credited to your account.*

Philippians 4:10–17

Promise 6: I promise to reach beyond any racial, ethnic, national, economic, political, or denominational barriers to demonstrate the power of biblical unity.

The Flame:

*For he himself is our peace, who has made the
two groups one and has destroyed the barrier, the
dividing wall of hostility.*

Ephesians 2:14

Be completely humble and gentle; be patient, bearing with one another in love. Make every effort to keep the unity of the Spirit through the bond of peace.

Ephesians 4:2–3

Promise 7: I promise to positively influence my world, and the greater world beyond, by being obedient to the Great Commandment.

The Flame:

Then Jesus came to them and said, "All authority in heaven and on earth has been given to me. Therefore go and make disciples of all nations, baptizing them in the name of the Father and of the Son and of the Holy Spirit, and teaching them to obey everything I have commanded you. And surely I am with you always, to the very end of the age."

Matthew 28:18–20

The Flame:

I press on to take hold of that for which Christ Jesus took hold of me.

Philippians 3:12

FIRE IT UP!

This is how I keep my promises:

_____

_____

_____

_____

_____

_____

_____

_____

My Passionate Prayer Time:

_____

_____

_____

_____

_____

_____

_____

_____

_____

23

Burning to Protect

Lord, I protect my wife and family with prayers throughout the day. I know, Lord, that this can be a negative world with the freezing rain of depression immobilizing them, or a dangerous world with the sun's heat of road rage attacking them on every street, or an apathetic world with a warm, soothing fog of complacency surrounding them and seducing them.

My family needs my umbrella of love over them, Lord, at all times to protect them from that rain, heat, or fog.

I pray that you would make my wife strong. Increase the strength in her spirit as mother, teacher, and counselor. She already has such boldness and love in teaching others your Word, beginning with our children. Give her more and more of that divine love and biblical boldness.

I pray for my children and grandchildren. Remind me, Lord, how children of all ages are drowning in a tsunami of temptations:

- Alcohol
- Drugs
- Facebook
- Internet dangers
- Bedroom on Wheels (a car)
- "Shoot-'em dead" video games with graphic violence and horrifying images
- Cell phones and iPods
- Sex-saturated music
- Television and movies

I pray for my children and I teach them the Five Ups:

1) "Wake UP! Watch where you're driving. No texting. Watch what you're eating and drinking. No fat burgers. No addictive energy shots."

2) "Shut UP! Please don't argue with me! I'm just trying to help you."

3) "Hang UP! Don't call her! Don't see her again; she's into drugs. Can't you see that?"

4) "Look UP! Your strength and direction come from God, not from your peers."

5) "Listen UP! Fill your mind only with the pure, positive, and powerful."

~

You said it, Lord: "The prayer of a righteous man has power."

I "listen up" to that promise, and I know I am righteous because of what Jesus did for me on the cross; therefore, as a sinner made righteous by your Son, I claim your power to protect my wife and family. Amen.

The Flame:

Anyone who does not provide for their relatives, and especially for their own household, has denied the faith and is worse than an unbeliever.

1 Timothy 5:8

FIRE IT UP!

This is how I protect my family:

_____

_____

_____

_____

_____

_____

_____

_____

My Passionate Prayer Time:

_____

_____

_____

_____

_____

_____

_____

_____

24

Burning to Eat Together

Lord, remind me of the statistics that demonstrate that the family that eats together stays together. (I know, Lord, it's also the family that prays together.)

So basic. So much fun.

Remind me of the joyous ritual: It starts with setting the table. In our home, we take turns. Someone pours the water or milk. Someone sets the silverware in place. Someone is stirring the gravy. Someone is laying out the napkins. Someone is rummaging through the back of the fridge to find the tub of butter. Then we sit and pray and dig in and talk. We sit at the table every night. We've learned to pray about people, not talk about people. Here at the table, we love to explore ideas. We talk about books and current events and people who need our help.

"There was this new kid at school today. I don't know where he came from, but he didn't like the teacher telling him to keep his eye on his book, so he told her to get lost."

"To say the least," I said, "that wasn't very discreet."

"What does discreet mean?" my daughter asks.

We keep a dictionary, a thesaurus, and a Bible in the middle of the table. "Shall we look up *Discreet?*"

"No, you look it up, honey," I encourage her.

Discreet. Comes from discern, which means to sift apart, or to examine.

"I guess that means, Dad, if that boy had thought about the trouble he'd get in for saying something so disrespectful, he would have shut up."

"Right. So, I tell you what. Let's pray for him," I suggest. (My daughter offers a quickie-prayer for a school buddy to have wisdom.)

"Pass the croissants, please, honey."

My lovely wife: "They're hot, hot, hot."

In the midst of silverware clanging against plates and glasses hitting the tabletop and the sound of forks scraping against teeth, I say, "Must be somebody kicking that boy's cat."

"What does that mean?" my son asks.

"Means, well, it means you're eaten up inside. You're hurting. You're feeling lonely or guilty or rejected. Somebody's been kicking your cat, and you take it out on others," I explain.

"Don't we do it around here sometimes? Mom, can I have some more corn? Don't we, well, when we're tired or in a bad mood, say things we shouldn't?"

"Whoops, I almost spilled that," I say as I catch the boat of salad dressing.

We talk about times when we've done stupid things, Lord. We talk about happy times, interrupting our chuckles with mouthfuls of squash and fish. We review those times we've blown up. No accusations. We're just talking. We're placing emotions on the table comfortably and casually, just like the plates we placed on the table.

Our kids are learning that **if you don't talk about emotions and control them, they control you.**

We talk,

and talk,

and talk,

surrounded by boiled cabbage, scalloped potatoes, chicken curry, pizza, mixed vegetables, brownies, or a variety of other foods, depending upon the night. We talk, we talk, and we talk.

Lord, remind me not to make a big speech about it, but once in a while, I'll slip it in: "You know, what we're doing is different these days. People used to do it all the time, but since television invaded the American home about seventy or so years ago, we have this strange and frightening phenomenon. People can sit in the same room, stare into the same blue haze, laugh at the same jokes, shriek at the same suspense, and cry at the same TV deaths for twenty years, and yet these strangers will split—because their eyes and ears and brains were fixed on the one-eyed seducer. It would be so simple to turn their heads toward each other and talk. Escape the blue haze and talk."

After dinner, we clean up together. Someone sweeps the floors, washes the dishes, and takes out the trash—together while talking.

We retreat to the living room for Bible reading, whether we feel like it or not. Each one prays. We have eaten of earthly food, now we digest your eternal food, Lord.

Lord, help me to keep this family ritual alive and growing. Keep this bond of love growing deeper by keeping us committed to eating dinner together. "Let's do it, family. Let's enjoy what the early Christians enjoyed when they talked about fellowship."

Lord, it reminds me of what Ronald Reagan said in his farewell address to the American people from the Oval Office in 1989: "All great change in America begins at the dinner table." Lord, I believe that with my whole heart. Amen.

The Flame:

They devoted themselves to the apostles' teaching and to fellowship, to the breaking of bread and to prayer.

Acts 2:42

FIRE IT UP!

This is what we can talk about while we eat together:

_____

_____

_____

_____

_____

_____

_____

_____

My Passionate Prayer Time:

_____

_____

_____

_____

_____

_____

_____

_____

_____

25

Burning to Toss

Thank you, Lord, for baseball and my backyard.

Never let me be too busy, Lord, to go out there and toss. There's something about grabbing my old mitt smelling of oil, dirt, and sandlot sweat—smooth 'n' soft from years on a diamond. Thank you for the thrill of hearing the hum, whoosh, and thump as it travels to Scotty and smacks his glove. Yeah, we're thirty feet apart, my son and I, but the toss and the thump tie us tight, Lord. I love it.

I wasn't much of a pitcher in my high school days, Lord, as you know. (Basketball was my game.) I got whacked a lot. None of that matters here. What matters is that Scotty knows he can throw problems to me.

"Dad, warm up first. Ready?"

"Always ready for you, son."

Hummmm.

Thump.

"Ow. Warm up?—that was heat!"

"Someone's getting old and soft."

"Let's see."

Hummmm.

Thump.

"Not bad, Dad."

Hummmm.

Thump.

"How are things going with Bridgett?"

Hummmm.

Thump.

"Saw her Saturday. Never saw her with this guy before, holding hands, walking around the park."

Hummmm.

Thump.

"So?"

Hummmm.

Thump.

"Woo—making me stretch with that one."

"So, she's my girl. It hurts."

"What? My pitch? Or the guy moving in?"

Hummmm.

Thump.

"Dad, you know what I mean."

Hummmm.

Thump.

"Remember when we talked about it at the café the other day after our workout? Here's the deal. There'll be some girls who like you that you don't like and vice versa. That's the deal. That's how it works. It's part of the sorting-out process."

Hummmm.

Thump.

"Still, she's my girl, Dad."

Hummmm.

Thump.

"At fourteen, Son? Move back a little. I'm going to smoke this one."

Whoooosh.

Thump.

"Call that 'smoke'!? Watch this."

Whoooosh.

Thump.

"Ow, again. You're too young to get serious, big guy. You've got a good brain, and you're a bundle of emotions like every teen is. Don't worry about having just <u>one</u> girlfriend. Have fun with lots of girls and guys in that group. Comes a pop fly. Let me see you shag it."

Hummmm.

Thump.

"Everyone kinda' pairs off and..."

Hummmm.

Thump.

"Looks that way sometimes, but I talked to your youth pastor, Brandon, and I know he encourages group things. 'Sides, he doesn't want you or Bridgett or anyone else to get hurt. Too young to get serious, Son. Could mess up a lot of things. Drop it."

Hummmm.

Thump.

"Drop what? The ball or Bridgett?"

Hummmm.

Thump.

"You know what I mean. Yeah, drop it. She'll figure it out. Remember what else I told you in the café? Like someone? Let them go. If they like you, they'll come back. If they don't come back, they didn't like you in the first place. And there are only about thirty-two other cool-looking chicks in that group. Give them the thrill of getting to know Super-Scotty."

Hummmm.

Thump.

"I see what you're saying."

Hummmm.

Thump.

"How's algebra? Ol' Dad's going to try a sinker. Squat down. Here it comes."

Hummm.

plop

plop

plop.

"Dad, I think you sank the sprinkler. Hit it dead on."

Hummmm.

Thump.

"You really know how to build a pitcher's ego. How's algebra?"

Hummmm.

Thump.

"Teacher's a jerk."

Hummmm.

Thump.

"What happened?"

Hummmm.

Thump.

"Grabbed my paper—everyone's—before we were done. Said I didn't show my work. B instead of an A."

Hummmm.

Thump.

"And? Hey, I'm going to hold it for a minute. Shoulder's getting stiff. And?"

"And, I went up to her desk, elbowed my way through the other kids, and said my work WAS <u>on the back</u>."

"Did she listen?"

"No."

"Did she hear you?"

"Had to."

"Obviously, I wasn't there. Sure she heard you? Surrounded by others?"

"Kinda."

"I'm for you Super Son, but maybe there's two or three things going on."

"Two or three what?"

"Teacher's got ego. Got to save face. Maybe it's precisely because she <u>did</u> hear you and didn't want to let on in front of the others. This the first time this happened?"

"Yeah."

"She's been a jerk before?"

"Not like this."

"I could go and talk to her, but you're a man. This is when you learn to talk without accusing, and I'm not talking about CON-FRON-TA-TION. Hate that word. Who needs to con-front anybody? Give them the benefit of the doubt, give them a chance to listen, give them a chance to speak. Move in a little. My shoulder's beginning to loosen up, finally."

Hummmm.

       Thump.

"She won't listen."

"Tried it, one-on-one?"

"Nooo."

Hummmm.

       Thump.

I stuffed the ball in the soft web, ripped the glove from my hand, shoved it under my armpit, and walked to my catcher.

"Try this. Tell her you'd like to see her after school for a few minutes. You want to apologize for something."

"Apologize? I didn't do any—"

"Just a minute. She won't be on the defensive. She'll be curious. Play the *I* game, not the *You* game."

"Whazit mean?"

"'Ms. Teacher, *I* am so sorry. *I* didn't realize how busy you were when *I* tried to show you my algebra. *I* should have waited until you didn't have a lot of other students around. May *I* ask you a question?' She'll say yes."

"Then?"

"Then you say, 'May I show you the back side of my algebra paper?' I'll bet you come up with a different outcome. Try it. Just try it, OK? We've got about forty-five minutes before dinner. Let's head to the park where we can whack a few. Dad's still got a few homers in him."

"Yeah. Thanks, Dad."

And, thank you, Lord, for the gift of toss. Amen.

The Flame:

Fathers, do not exasperate your children; instead, bring them up in the training and instruction of the Lord.

Ephesians 6:4

FIRE IT UP!

This is how I toss with my son or daughter:

_____

_____

_____

_____

_____

_____

_____

_____

My Passionate Prayer Time:

_____

_____

_____

_____

_____

_____

_____

_____

26

Burning to Tell My Family the Five Wishes

Lord, help me to let my family know what my final wishes are—You know, the ones I teach in my seminars? (Hey, if I am going to preach it, I better practice it.)

Give me the candor and consideration to tell them. You know that I don't want to procrastinate on this important task; I do not presume that they already know: I want to tell them to KNOW with my mouth and on paper what my wishes are BEFORE I get sick, injured, or die. I do not want to leave the stress and burden of those critical decisions to any family member. That's cruel.

I remember, Lord, those three sisters and two brothers circled around the hospital bed of Pops, who was gasping with oxygen tubes and struggling with needles puncturing him until he looked like a cactus.

The kids were arguing about whether to remove life support. Pops told me in an earlier counseling session about his estate-planning wishes. But he never got around to writing it down.

Didn't the kids know that the last sense to go is hearing? Pops heard all the fighting and fussing. He should have been hearing someone reciting Psalm 23 or John 14 or the words of a prayer for your peace. He should have heard the words "I love you, Pops."

And then, Lord, remember there was that sixty-year-old daughter standing at the hospice bed of Momma. Momma was shaking in pain from the leukemia ravaging her body, but the daughter said, "No, nurse. Don't give her morphine. I don't think Momma would ever want to be a drug addict."

"Drug addict, what are you thinking, lady? Your momma is dying and besides Momma told me! She told me in her office, but she never wrote it down. 'Give me whatever medicine I need to keep me comfortable.'"

It's in the *Five Wishes*.

Help me again, Lord, to tell by mouth and by document, what my FIVE WISHES are and to inspire others to do the same:

WISH 1:

The person I want to make health care decisions for me when I can't make them for myself.

If I am no longer able to make my own health care decisions, this form names the person I choose to make these choices for me. This person will be my Health Care Agent or other term that may be used in my state, such as proxy, representative, or surrogate. This person will make my health care choices if both of these things happen:

- My attending or treating doctor finds I am no longer able to make health care choices, AND
- Another health care professional agrees that this is true.

The person I choose as my health care agent is:

_____   _____
First-Choice Name   Phone

_____
Address

_____   _____   _____
City   State   Zip

If this person is not able or willing to make these choices for me, OR is divorced or legally separated from me, OR this person has died, then these people are my next choices:

_____   _____
Second-Choice Name   Phone

_____
Address

_____   _____   _____
City   State   Zip

_____   _____
Third-Choice Name   Phone

_____
Address

_____ _____ _____
City   State   Zip

WISH 2:

My wish for the kind of medical treatment I want or don't want:
I believe that my life is precious, and I deserve to be treated
with dignity. When the time comes that I am very sick and am
not able to speak for myself, I want the following wishes, and
any other directions I have given to my Health Care Agent, to
be respected and followed.

What you should keep in mind as my caregiver:

- I do not want to be in pain. I want my doctor to give me
  enough medicine to relieve my pain, even if that means that
  I will be drowsy or sleep more than I would otherwise.
- I do not want anything done or omitted by my doctors or
  nurses with the intention of taking my life.
- I want to be offered food and fluids by mouth and kept clean
  and warm.

What "Life-Support Treatment" means to me:
Life-support treatment means any medical procedure, device,
or medication to keep me alive. Life-support treatment includes:

medical devices that may help me to breathe, eat, and drink supplied by a medical device (tube feeding); cardiopulmonary resuscitation (CPR); major surgery; blood transfusions; dialysis; antibiotics; and anything else meant to keep me alive. If I wish to limit the meaning of life-support treatment because of my religious or personal beliefs, I write this limitation in the space below. I do this to make very clear what I want and under what conditions.

_____

_____

_____

_____

_____

_____

Here is the kind of medical treatment that I want or don't want in the four situations listed below. I want my Health Care Agent, my family, my doctors and other health care providers, my friends, and all others to know these directions.

(1) Close to death:

If my doctor and another health care professional both decide that I am likely to die within a short period of time, and life-support treatment would only delay the moment of my death (Choose *one* of the following):

☐ I want to have life-support treatment.

☐ I do not want life-support treatment. If it has been started, I want it stopped.

☐ I want to have life-support treatment if my doctor believes it could help. But I want my doctor to stop giving me life-support treatment if it is not helping my health condition or symptoms.

(2) In a coma and not expected to wake up or recover:

If my doctor and another health care professional both decide that I am in a coma from which I am not expected to wake up or recover, and I have brain damage, and life-support treatment would only delay the moment of my death (Choose *one* of the following):

☐ I want to have life-support treatment.

☐ I do not want life-support treatment. If it has been started, I want it stopped.

☐ I want to have life-support treatment if my doctor believes it could help. But I want my doctor to stop giving me life-support treatment if it is not helping my health condition or symptoms.

(3) Permanent and severe brain damage and not expected to recover:

If my doctor and another health care professional both decide that I have permanent and severe brain damage, (for example), I can open my eyes, but I cannot speak or understand, and I am not expected to get better, and life-support treatment would only delay the moment of my death (Choose *one* of the following):

☐ I want to have life-support treatment.

☐ I do not want life-support treatment. If it has been started, I want it stopped.

☐ I want to have life-support treatment if my doctor believes it could help. But I want my doctor to stop giving me life-support treatment if it is not helping my health condition or symptoms.

(4) In another condition under which I do not wish to be kept alive:

If there is another condition under which I do not wish to have life-support treatment, I describe it below. In this condition, I believe that the costs and burdens of life-support treatment are too much and are not worth the benefits to me. Therefore, in this condition, I do not want life-support treatment. (For example, you may write "end-stage condition." That means that your health has gotten worse. You are not able to take care of yourself in any way, mentally or physically. Life-support treatment will not help you recover. Please leave the space blank if you have no other condition to describe.)

_____

_____

_____

_____

_____

_____

WISH 3:

My wish for how comfortable I want to be:

- I do not want to be in pain. I want my doctor to give me enough medicine to relieve my pain, even if that means I will be drowsy and sleep more than I would otherwise.
- If I show signs of depression, nausea, shortness of breath, or hallucinations, I want my caregivers to do whatever they can to help me.
- I wish to have a cool, moist cloth put on my head if I have a fever.
- I want my lips and mouth kept moist to stop the dryness.
- I wish to have warm baths often. I wish to be kept fresh and cool at all times.
- I wish to be massaged with warm oils as often as I can be.
- I wish to have my favorite music played when possible until my time of death. This music includes:

_____

_____

_____

_____

_____

- I wish to have personal care like shaving, nail clipping, hair brushing, and teeth brushing, as long as they do not cause me pain or discomfort.
- I wish to have the Bible read to me, especially these verses:

_____

_____

_____

_____

_____

WISH 4:

My wish for how I want people to treat me:

- I wish to have people with me when possible. I want someone to be with me when it seems that death may come at any time.
- I wish to have my hand held and to be talked to when possible, even if I don't seem to respond to the voice or touch of others.
- I wish to have others by my side praying for me when possible.
- I wish to have the members of my church or synagogue told that I am sick and asked to pray for me and visit me.
- I wish to be cared for with kindness and cheerfulness, not sadness.
- I wish to have pictures of my loved ones in my room, near my bed.

- If I am not able to control my bowel or bladder functions, I wish for my clothes and bed linens to be kept clean, and for them to be changed as soon as they can be if they have been soiled.
- I want to die in my home, if that can be done.

WISH 5:

My wish for what I want my loved ones to know:

- I wish to have my family and friends know that I love them.
- I wish to be forgiven for the times I have hurt my family, friends, and others.
- I wish to have my family, friends, and others know that I forgive them for when they may have hurt me in my life.
- I wish for my family and friends to know that I do not fear death itself. I think it is not the end, but a new beginning for me.
- I wish for all my family members to make peace with each other before my death, if they can.
- I wish for my family and friends to think about what I was like before I became seriously ill. I want them to remember me in this way after my death.
- I wish for my family and friends and caregivers to respect my wishes, even if they don't agree with them.

Help me, Lord, to make certain my family knows my five wishes, and then help countless more people do the same before they die. Amen.

The Flame:

Anyone who does not provide for their relatives and especially for their own household has denied the faith and is worse than an unbeliever.

1 Timothy 5:8

Honor your father and mother, and love your neighbor as yourself.

Matthew 19:19

FIRE IT UP!

Here's a draft of my Five Wishes:

_____

_____

_____

_____

_____

_____

_____

My Passionate Prayer Time:

_____

_____

_____

_____

_____

_____

_____

Burning for Others

27

Burning to be Approachable

Lord, who's calling me at 2:57 in the morning?

"Doc, Annie's in jail."

"Whozis?"

"We need $1,650 for the bail bondsman to get her out."

"Wha—What are you talking about? Bail? Jail? Whozis?" Words stumbled out of my mouth like dry cotton balls stuck in my gums.

"Derek, Derek, Annie's husband. She thought a very old DWI was erased from the record, but it's like it was never taken care of, so on her record it looks like she tried to skip it."

"Wait, wait, wait. Who IS this?" I sit on the side of the bed and fumble for the lamp. I see my toes dangle above the carpet. I hold the phone away from my ear and see the black letters "Derek" shining from the green background of my phone screen.

"We need $1,650 for the bail bondsman." He fires words into my ear like bullets from an Uzi. "She was stopped for speeding last night, and when they pulled up the license, they saw this outstanding warrant, handcuffed her, and threw her in jail. I'm here with Bella. She's asleep, and she doesn't know that her mama is in jail. I KNOW we took care of that ticket a long time ago."

"What are you calling me for, Derek? Go down there. Call Annie's parents. That makes more sense."

"I don't know if they've got the money or not, but Annie doesn't want her parents to know anyway. *Besides I can't leave Bella.*"

He's calling me because he's broke. Derek's calling me because he doesn't have $1,650 to put together. Derek's not calling his parents because of embarrassment. Why me?

"I'll call you back," I say.

What's he calling me for? (My mind is still in the Twilight Zone.) *He doesn't have $1,650, his wife's in jail, and they don't want the family to know. But why me? Was Jesus this approachable? Are Christians supposed to be this accessible? A sucker or a servant? He could take Bella with him. He could.*

I remembered a couple of passages from my Bible reading earlier that day. Jesus let his friends poke him while he was asleep in the boat. On another occasion, he invited kids to climb all over him, tired as he was. He even let Judas betray him for a bigger purpose.

I called Derek: "Go to the bondsman's office; I'll meet you there with a check."

Lord, while I was driving back from the bondsman's office, at 4:45 a.m., it hit me: *Millions are like Derek, aren't they Lord? They just want to be helped UNCONDITIONALLY. Millions—at a time of crisis, shame, or fear—well, they don't need a lecture, a scolding, or an interrogation. They just need help, with skin and sweat on it. Whether it is*

- *Emotional*
- *Financial*
- *Physical*
- *Spiritual*

"Help me."

I think I get it, Lord. Strange, even those closest to Jesus sometimes didn't get it, did they?

Jesus's followers shooed the children away like swatting flies around a pie: "Don't bother us. Don't bother Jesus."

And when aroused in the boat, Jesus did not say, "I'm tired. Lemme' go back to sleep. You take care of the boat." No, no, no. "I'm approachable," Jesus said. "I care about people. Let the children come to me."

Jesus showed us that one's soul is healed and spirit lifted by being with children and by being *childlike*.

The woman with the bleeding problem heard that Jesus was *approachable*. She put Jesus to the test by elbowing her way through a hostile crowd. *Lady, get in line. Quit your shoving.* And she continued to lunge forward like a fullback eyeballing the goal line three yards away. She pushed, and shoved, and touched his robe. And he loved her and healed her.

The woman who washed Jesus's feet with her hair—what a good hair day that was for her (sorry for the quip, Lord). She believed; she hoped that Jesus was approachable. She was right. And she was comforted, commended, and forgiven.

Remind me, Lord, that the Christian life is NOT a life of ease, comfort, convenience, or popularity. It's a life of radical caring, isn't it? A life that lets people know they can come.

Come.

Come.

Come.

Come. Isn't that what you said, Lord? "Come unto me. Come unto me and I will give you rest."

Lord, it's 5:36 in the morning. I'm back home. I still wonder if I have been suckered in.

So what.

I'm glad that Derek called, Lord. I'm also grateful that Annie and Derek and Bella are home. Thank you for showing me again, Lord, that the Christian heart and the Christian home are always open to everyone. Or open to no one. Amen.

The Flame:

Jesus said, "Let the little children come to me, and do not hinder them, for the kingdom of heaven belongs to such as these."

Matthew 19:14

FIRE IT UP!

This is how I will be more approachable:

_____

_____

_____

_____

_____

_____

_____

_____

My Passionate Prayer Time:

_____

_____

_____

_____

_____

_____

_____

_____

28

Burning to Love

Love a cold Gatorade. Love to watch 'da Boys win on Sunday. Love shooting hoops with my son and daughter. Love to cook. Love chocolate chip cookies warm from the oven. Love to watch the sun melt below the horizon of the ocean, pink and purple fading with a flare. Love the aroma of sizzling bacon in the morning.

Soooooooooo, what's this love they're talking about, Lord?

Lord, I want to burn with the love YOU show. Not this touchy-feely stuff tickling our senses. I applaud you that you made us to give and receive love unconditionally. That's what makes us new, better, and different. We are your creation of love, radiating your passion and personality.

And we learn quickly, don't we, that in this life, Lord, that when we need this God-type of love, UNCONDITIONAL LOVE, we need it now.

No excuses, please.

I'm hurting.

I'm scared.

I'm desperate.

Don't tell me it's uncomfortable, inconvenient, embarrassing, time consuming, too radical, or too costly.

Of course, it's costly because it's God's love.

And it's UNCONDITIONAL because it's God's love.

Her name was Toni. (Remember, Lord?)

I walked in my office building that Tuesday morning and saw her slumped on the leather couch by the elevator. I saw her shoulders heaving up and down in cadence with her shrieks and sobs. *Not anyone working in this building, I don't think. Never seen her before.*

I lifted the sharp-angled white handkerchief from my breast pocket and extended it to her. "May I be so intrusive and ask if there's anything I can do to help? Take this, please, ma'am." I snapped the handkerchief open and shook it to its full length, now a hand towel.

"I'll never see him again. Never. I'll never . . ."

"Who?"

"My son."

"Did you have an accident? Did your s—? May I sit down?"

"No, upstairs. His lawyer said, 'Get used to it. Jason's his.'"

"'His'? Who?"

"My boyfriend. We've split. He took Jason."

"Jason's your s-son? I'm guessing here."

"Yes. Mario is my boyfriend. Might still be up there in the lawyer's office. Got to the daycare before I did." Her cell phone rang. "No, Mom. No, Mom. I can't talk now. I can't. I'll call you back."

This is moving too fast. Where is this going?

"I'm still guessing. Mario went to daycare? Got there before you did and got Jason out and then took him what—to his house? And then got this lawyer to stonewall you? Something like that?"

"Yes, we were together again just a few days. Mario hit me, slapped Jason around, and left. Said he'd get even."

"Get even for what?"

"Drunks don't need reasons," she snapped and sat up. "What do you care? Who are you?"

"Do you want help or not? Do you have custody?" I asked, flipping my wrist over and staring at my watch.

Do I have time for this?

"Custody? What for? Mario's just a boyfriend. Used to be. Been living in and out for a few years. Left a note for me at the daycare. 'Go see lawyer.'"

I looked at my watch again: 10:14 a.m. My clients had been waiting upstairs since 10:00 a.m. I flipped my cell phone open and stabbed the speed dial for my office. "Laura, I assume Dr. and Mrs. Wells are still there? I'll be there, honestly; I'll be there real quick. Put in that DVD of *America's Greatest Moments*. Tell them I apologize. Five minutes. Five minutes. Yes, I know, I know. They've waited two and a half months for this appointment. I know. They've got the $750,000 (401k) paperwork. I know. I know."

I returned to Toni.

"Do you have a lawyer, Toni?"

"It won't do any good. The lawyer upstairs said he's got him, and he's moving out of the state, maybe already did. I don't know what Mario told that lawyer."

I flipped my cell phone again and called my attorney. "Tyrone, do you know a good family lawyer?"

"David Walsh. Here's his number."

I hit the red button, ending the call. I hit the green button and dialed in David Walsh's number.

Got him.

I briefed him and he asked me to put Toni on the phone. She exploded into sobs and spit out the facts. She handed the phone back to me.

"I need a $3,500 retainer to get this started. Send her over. We'll see what we can do. If she's telling the truth, we can help her and need to do it immediately before this guy gets too far."

Did he say $3,500? I don't even know this woman.

"Stay here, Toni."

I ran upstairs, praying all the time. I escorted Dr. and Mrs. Wells to a conference room with profuse apologies. "I'll be right back."

I wrote a check to attorney David Walsh, stuffed it in a sealed envelope, and handed it to my assistant Laura. "Laura, there's a gal downstairs by the elevator; her name is Toni. Give her this envelope, point out to her that on the front I've put David Walsh's name and address. She has already talked to him. She knows who he is. She's going to take this to him."

I met with Dr. and Mrs. Wells, fulfilled my appointment, accepted their paperwork, and handed them their one-inch-thick estate plan, including a revocable living trust, showing how their three-quarter million dollars was being put to work for growth, income, and legacy planning.

Thank you, Lord.

At 2:50 p.m., I receive a call from David Walsh's office. "I talked to Toni. We sent Child Protective Services and the Dallas police to make a little visit to Mario. Essentially, Mario kidnapped Jason. Toni's got Jason back. Mario's in a holding tank, and he'll probably be there for a while. He won't harass Toni again."

Thank you, Lord, for your victory.

And Toni never talked to me again. I never heard from her. No call. No visit. No "thank you."

And I know why.

Lord, you are some royal ruler and a royal rascal. You set that up. You sent Toni like an angel to me, like you sent the angel to wrestle with Jacob. You wanted her to get help, yes, but you also wanted to wrestle with my faith. You wanted to see if I was going to walk the talk.

Earlier that day, Lord, you remember I started by saying, "Lord, make my life a miracle of your service." (WARNING:

NEVER pray that prayer unless you mean it and you're ready for a rollercoaster ride of belly-churning risks, scary decisions, and divine victories.)

I'm burning to love, Lord, like you love.

Feed my fire.

Lord, you know I've been given ties, books, DVDs, sports bottles, but one of the most treasured Father's Day gifts was the one I received from my son, Matthew. That gift could have been from any of my kids because they've adorned me with these sentiments before. Totally undeserved but totally appreciated.

Matthew put it in writing. He quoted the song sung by Clay Davidson, "Unconditional":

> You can't stop my love to you.
> It will be here, that's a given;
> As long as I am living on this Earth;
> One thing is true;
> You could turn away, forget me;
> Curse my name,
> But love won't let me let you go.
> Son, always know
> My love is unconditional.

("Unconditional," single sung by Clay Davidson written by Rivers Rutherford, Deanna Bryant, Liz Hengber from *Unconditional,* Virgin Records, 2000. Used by permission.)

And then Matthew ended: "Dad, thanks for your

unconditional love to me and to the family."

If this page in this book is spotted, it is because my ping-pong-ball-sized tears are splashed all over it, after rereading Matthew's note as I write.

Thank you, Lord, for the test of Toni. Thank you for your unconditional love. Giving it, receiving it. That is what the world needs now, Lord. Amen.

And walk in the way of love, just as Christ loved us and gave himself up for us as a fragrant offering and sacrifice to God.

Ephesians 5:2

Dear friends, let us love one another, for love comes from God. Everyone who loves has been born of God and knows God.

1 John 4:7

The Flame:

Place me like a seal over your heart, like a seal on your arm; for love is as strong as death, its jealousy unyielding as the grave. It burns like blazing fire, like a mighty flame.

Song of Songs 8:6

FIRE IT UP!

This is how I love unconditionally:

_____

_____

_____

_____

_____

_____

_____

_____

My Passionate Prayer Time:

_____

_____

_____

_____

_____

_____

_____

_____

_____

29

Burning to Build

They're blasting Texas Stadium, Lord, right in front of me. I and thousands of others sit jammed along Airport Freeway to gawk—some to cry—at this historic event at 7:00 a.m. Sunday morning.

Twenty-eight years of the glory of Tom Landry, Roger Staubach, Troy Aikman, Drew Pearson, Too Tall Jones, Emmitt Smith, Bob Lily all in twenty-five seconds.

Bam!

Wham!

Sunk.

Gone.

Now it's looking like a pregnant woman lying on her back—just a shakin' and quiverin' mound. There are visible pains of labor, but no new birth here.

Quite the opposite.

It was so easy, so quick, yet so painful to watch it collapse.

Meanwhile, south on Highway 360 in Arlington, sixteen miles from here, they're lifting beams to build the "Texas Temple" (per the locals). Officially, they'll call it Cowboys Stadium, the 1.1-billion-dollar crown of glory to Jerry Jones and his platoon of Sunday warriors.

It was easy to blast Texas Stadium. Twenty-five seconds. It took much more effort to build Cowboys Stadium. Twenty-five months of planning, financing, digging, building, and lifting, all dedicated to erect this edifice of athletics.

Lord, build in me the passion to build people like they're building stadiums. Whack me in the head when I'm tempted to bomb their dress, motives, actions, or words. It's so easy, so ego satisfying to believe the worst. Build in me, Lord, the habit of building and lifting, not bombing and criticizing.

An elevator? What's this picture of an elevator in my head, Lord? What's that got to do with?

Oh, I see. I hit ↑ and it goes up, and I hit ↓ and it goes down. Let me try it with my tongue, Lord. I unfurl my tongue, aim its tip, and hit ↑. It goes up.

Ready, aim. I unfurl my tongue, aim, hit ↓. It goes down.

I see: That's what I do all day long with my tongue. I lift people up, or I push them down. I build them, or I blast them.

And, Lord, protect me from using my tongue for flattery. That's phony and cunning. That's not lifting. That's lying.

I will use it for praise. That's lifting. That's loving.

And help me as I approach each person, Lord, to see stamped on each person's forehead MMFS: Make Me Feel Special.

Remind me, Lord, that everyone's having a tough day. Empower me to be gentle and to look directly into their eyes when I ask, "How are you doing?" so that each person knows that I want to build him or her up. "This is the place and this is the time. If you need to talk, there's someone who cares and listens."

With my eyes, I invite. With my ears, I listen. With my tongue, I lift. And, with my energy, I build.

Let me not be so naïve, Lord, to think that every person is secure, composed, or impenetrable. You've made us, Lord, to love and be loved.

CEO or homeless beggar, tycoon or toddler, athlete or cripple, student or teacher, I've got the tongue, and I've got the power to lift their burdens and to build their hopes.

Thank you, Lord, for your words of life.

> *A person finds joy in giving an apt reply—and how good is a timely word!*
>
> Proverbs 15:23

Oh and thank you, Lord, for that interview with Truett Cathy. As I sat behind his massive desk in his tree-house office, at Chick-Fil-A headquarters in Atlanta, he looked at me and said (with that Santa Claus twinkle):

"Now, I've got a question for you, Dr. Gallagher."

"And that is?" I replied.

"How can you tell if a person needs encouragement?"

"How?" I ask.

"If he is still breathing," he answered with a smile.

The Flame:

Light in the messenger's eyes brings joy to the heart, and good news gives health to the bones.

Proverbs 15:30

FIRE IT UP!

This is how I build people with my words:

_____

_____

_____

_____

_____

_____

_____

My Passionate Prayer Time:

_____

_____

_____

_____

_____

_____

_____

30

Burning to Cry

With others. Lord.

I'm not looking forward to it. Who does? But when the time comes, fill me with the compassion of Jesus. Deliver me from timidity, hesitation, or outright refusal.

I've heard the thousands who say (and I sympathize with them), "I don't visit nursing homes. I don't do funerals. I don't go to hospitals."

Like the cold corpse and his grieving family are experts at doing funerals? Like the cancerous husband and his worried wife stuck in a hospital have doctorates in hope, comfort, and courage?

Remind me, Lord, that when you give us the opportunity to serve, you also give us the ability.

Thank you for allowing me, Father, to have that interview with writer Joseph Bayly. Now, there's a guy who knows something about grieving and about ministering to those who are grieving. He lost three sons.

I remember him saying there are three types of people, three types at your time of need:

1) Those who refused to come. Bad.

2) Those who come and blab. Lectures on the Book of Job, tales of pain and woe from their own tragedies. Blather. Blather. Blather. But at least they came. Better.

3) Those who came and sat. Best. "They just sat with me. Occasionally put an arm around me, held my hand, maybe a short prayer, but they came and sat. We cried and reminisced. But mainly sat. I missed them the most when they left."

Give me patience, Lord, with those who say, "I don't do times of grief." Remind me to take those folks with me when I go on my visits. (Hey, I need help as much as they do.)

They'll see that

- You don't need theological answers.
- You don't need counseling skills.
- You don't have to explain or defend God.
- You don't need professional words of advice.

They'll feel the heart of Mr. Grieving or Ms. Worried: it's a heart that's ripped and bleeding. They'll know that Mr. Grieving or Ms. Worried NEEDS a heart within skin distance where there's a transfusion of hope and love and strength.

BE THERE.

That's how you do funerals, hospitals, and nursing homes.

Just be there.

And remind me next time, Lord, to slip my slim Bible in my pocket. Last time I went, I sensed the time was right for me to share a word from Psalm 23 or Romans 8 or John 3. But I wasn't ready. I'll be ready next time.

And thank you, Lord, for the opportunity to point out that the glamorous folks like Barbara Streisand are wrong: "People Who Need People Are the Luckiest People in the World." (Her signature song.)

No!

Help me to smash these glamorous and cultural clichés that showcase half-truths about love, support, and comfort, which are no truths at all.

PEOPLE WHO NEED PEOPLE ARE THE ONLY PEOPLE IN THE WORLD.

Remind us, Lord, that as your man or your woman, we don't have the luxury of self-pity EVER and that is because other people need us. They need us to just be there. Like you always are, Lord.

The Flame:

Blessed are those who mourn, for they will be comforted.

Matthew 5:4

Rejoice with those who rejoice; mourn with those who mourn.

Romans 12:15

FIRE IT UP!

This is how I grieve and help others to grieve:

_____

_____

_____

_____

_____

_____

_____

_____

My Passionate Prayer Time:

_____

_____

_____

_____

_____

_____

_____

_____

31

Burning to Help Richard

Doctor or doorman, we want to hide our hurts, Lord. Too proud. Too shy. Too scared to tell others our needs.

So help me, Lord, to pierce that shield of fear, pride, or secrecy.

We've all heard this:

"The Whites are getting a divorce? Can't be. Been neighbors for eighteen years. I thought everything was great."

"What? Ortiz's son has run away? He used to be in my Sunday school class. Juan never gave me a clue."

"Nelson's having surgery tomorrow? Tomorrow? Tumor? Brain? Knew a year ago? Why didn't he tell us?"

Lord, help me to pierce the Richards of the world (wherever they are) and to LOOK at Richard (whoever he is) and to ask genuine questions.

Not just "How're you doing?", "Fine," and that's it.

No! No! No!

Ask sincere and loving questions. Then shut up and listen, allowing him (or her) to talk, talk, talk.

Before it's too late. I recall Edward Arlington Robinson's haunting narrative poem:

Whenever Richard Cory went downtown,
We people on the pavement looked at him:
He was a gentleman from sole to crown,
Clean favored, and imperially slim.

And he was always quietly arrayed,
And he was always human when he talked;
But still he fluttered pulses when he said,
"Good-morning," and he glittered when he walked.

And he was rich—yes, richer than a king—
And admirably schooled in every grace:
In fine we thought that he was everything,
To make us wish that we were in his place.

So on we worked, and waited for the light,
And went without the meat and cursed the bread;
And Richard Cory, one calm summer night,
Went home and put a bullet through his head.

(Edwin Arlington Robinson, "Richard Cory," in *The Children of the Night*, 1847.)

Lord, I've learned enough to know that you do answer prayer. Thank you, Lord.

My prayer: "Help me to see people as you see them."

Help me to say the words you would say to my neighbor, colleague, librarian, waitress, mechanic, whomever.

How about if I start with this: "Anything you want to talk about? Anything I can help you with?" Or maybe I just say, "How's your day?" And then when they reply, I'll say, "I understand. You know, there IS a way to make every day a great day regardless of what other people say, think, or do. Do you want to hear about it?"

Maybe that's the time to introduce them to your heavenly perspective.

For God so loved the world that he gave his one and only Son, that whoever believes in him shall not perish but have eternal life.

John 3:16

Since, then, you have been raised with Christ, set your hearts on things above, where Christ is, seated at the right hand of God. Set your minds on things above, not on earthly things.

Colossians 3:1–2

Jesus looked at them and said, "With man this is impossible, but with God all things are possible."

Matthew 19:26

Cross references:
Matthew 19:26 : Ge 18:14; Job 42:2; Jer 32:17; Lk 1:37; 18:27; Ro 4:21

Then I'll just wait. Perhaps, I'll give them my phone number. They may not talk then, but I'll let them know there's somebody out there who will listen.

People all around me are boiling with something inside, aren't they, Lord?

Everyone's looking for someone who cares. Isn't that the way you made us, Lord? Help me to be there at the right time, with your gracious words. Amen.

The Flame:

Carry each other's burdens and in this way you will fulfill the law of Christ.

Galatians 6:2

We who are strong ought to bear with the failings of the weak and not to please ourselves.

Romans 15:1

FIRE IT UP!

This is how I help Richard and others like him:

_____

_____

_____

_____

_____

_____

_____

_____

My Passionate Prayer Time:

_____

_____

_____

_____

_____

_____

_____

_____

32

Burning to Forgive

Thank you, Lord, for showing me that when I hate, I force another to own me.

I didn't get that at first.

"Own me?"

I hate him, so how does he own me? Five ways:

1. I delight in designing ways to hurt him.
2. I daydream about strategies to get even. I plot revenge.
3. I taste the sweetness of the moment when I crush him.
4. He screams for mercy. "I'm sorry, I'm sorry, I'm sorry."
5. I gloat in his fear and pain.

"I ... him."

"I ... him."

"I ... him."

I am obsessed by him. He owns me. He becomes the master; I am the slave.

I replay mental recordings:

"How could he have done that to me?"

"I trusted her and she betrayed me."

"He lied to me. Lied to me!"

"Never realized she was setting me up the whole time."

"I'll never get over this."

"I ... him."

"I ... him."

"I ... him."

"I ... her."

"I ... her."

"I ... her."

Over and over, I replay the words. The repeated message of hate scars my brain and sprays poison into the freshly etched grooves.

Poison?

That's it.

When I choose to hate, it's like choosing to drink poison, isn't it, Lord? I'm drinking the poison while hoping that *he'll* get sick and die.

I'm the one getting sick!

What? Forgive him? Big Al? C'mon, Lord. Give me a break. None of this applies to me.

Lord, don't you remember what Big Al did to me? Surely, you remember:

Big Al suffered a mild heart attack. I granted him time off from work. Lots of time. With pay, no questions asked.

No labor law said I had to do it. I wanted to help the guy. I appreciated him and trusted him and told him so.

He returned to work and wanted to build a property business of his own. No problem. Go ahead and use the Gallagher Financial fax, copier, phones, and computers. I'll use my radio show and seminars and television appearances to promote your business.

I don't want a dime.

I then discovered Big Al was setting me up and stealing files, records, and passwords. He assumed I was an amiable dunce, inept, and naïve.

What kind of a business leader—especially in the competitive area of financial services—puts his employees' needs above his own? What kind of a boss gives an employee weeks off with pay no questions asked? Big Al had seen me do it for others.

"Of course, he'll do it for me; what a dummy Doc is."

You remember, Lord, he conspired with three others to steal my records, torch my business, trash my reputation, and open his own office.

Caught him, fired him.

Too late.

Somehow he slithered in, grabbed hundreds of files, smashed my computers, and called clients to scream the Big Lie: "I couldn't stand Gallagher's business practices anymore, and so I decided to quit. Would you like to transfer your account to me?"

Razor went from Adam's apple to aorta: He called state regulators to "report" me for alleged fraud and concocted violations. (Smart move: that'll tie you up for months, if not years.)

Regulators, you and I discovered, Lord, well, they love to hear from disgruntled employees. They've got scripts ready for these malcontents to recite, thereby dumping revenge on their former bosses.

Thousands of productive work hours lost, wasted in hearings and depositions.

Thousands of dollars in legal bills to produce records and defend my innocence against Big Al's charges. ("Defend my innocence?" For <u>what</u>? I didn't do anything.)

My innocence doesn't matter. With some crusading regulators, the attitude is, "Don't confuse me with the facts."

If they can't find a bad guy, they'll create one.

Reminded me, Lord, of that travesty with the Duke University students and the crusading DA? In that case, the crusader turned out to be criminal. That attorney, in his zeal, censored exculpatory evidence and created condemnatory evidence. Mercifully for the Duke students and their families, the DA got caught, lost his law license, and was thrown in the slammer.

That regulator got deregulated, defrocked, and detained behind bars.

What am I going to do about the regulators that Big Al unleashed on me?

"I'm going to be wiped out," I thought. "This is too big an assault. God, this is W-A-Y too big. How do I go home and tell Gail the business is about to be smashed and gone?"

Years of struggle, thousands of appointments, a hundred thousand disappointments, delays, and rejections. Millions of risk capital put to work to build a financial-consulting business. Thousands of clients needed me and trusted me.

I wanted to melt in despair and smash Big Al's face in hate and fury.

I screamed with rage and cried out in panic, "I'll get him."

Then I remembered Corrie Ten Boom.

Corrie's story hit me like a hammer smacking my forehead:

> It was a church service in Munich that I saw him, the former SS man who had stood guard at the shower room door in the processing center at Ravensbrück. He was the first of our actual jailers that I had seen since that time. And suddenly it was all there—the roomful of mocking men, the heaps of clothing, Betsie's pain-blanched face.
>
> He came up to me as the church was emptying, beaming and bowing. "How grateful I am for your message, Fräulein," he said. "To think that, as you say, He has washed my sins away!"
>
> His hand was thrust out to shake mine. And I, who had preached so often to the people in

Bloemendaal the need to forgive, kept my hand at my side.

Even as the angry, vengeful thoughts boiled through me, I saw the sin of them. Jesus Christ had died for this man; was I going to ask for more? Lord Jesus, I prayed, forgive me and help me to forgive him.

I tried to smile. I struggled to raise my hand. It was impossible. I felt nothing, not the slightest spark of warmth or charity. And so again I breathed a silent prayer. Jesus, I cannot forgive him. Give your forgiveness.

As I took his hand the most incredible thing happened. From my shoulder along my arm and through my hand, a current seemed to pass from me to him, while into my heart sprang a love for this stranger that almost overwhelmed me.

And so I discovered that it is not on our forgiveness any more than on our goodness that the world's healing hinges, but on His.

I sank to my knees and I prayed forgiveness and grace over Big Al, repenting of my hate and releasing the poison in me. The fire of hate and revenge was replaced by grace and forgiveness and an amazing thing happened. I was set free. I was healed of hate.

Thank you, Lord.

Not only did I feel the poison drain from my soul, but I saw victory triumph. Regulators left me alone. I was exonerated from Big Al's accusations. I rebuilt my business so it was bigger and better.

Victory came to the point where I received a proclamation from the governor thanking me and my company for our compassionate and practical work helping investors, particularly seniors. Ours is the only financial firm in Texas to receive such a proclamation.

I wrote the popular *The Money Doctor's Guide to Taking Care of Yourself When No One Else Will*. I am now (Thank you, Lord) a columnist for *Bottom Line*, the nation's leading financial bulletin. I am featured with Jack Canfield (of *Chicken Soup* fame) on the CD series "Strategies for Excellence." I am the financial speaker for Zig Ziglar's *Born to Win* seminars, and our practice continues to flourish.

The serendipity of this for clients and for me was that a few years ago, when 40 million Americans lost 50 percent or more in their brokerage accounts, 401ks, and retirement plans, our clients lost nothing. Thank you, Lord, for all of that.

And I gained everything by learning to forgive. Thank you, Lord, for the freedom of forgiveness. Twice blessed: He who forgives is forgiven.

STATE OF TEXAS
OFFICE OF THE GOVERNOR

Greetings:

As Governor of Texas, I am pleased to extend greetings to all in attendance at the annual North Texas Expo on Aging *Celebrating Life*

Senior Texans have cared for families and communities, enhanced economic prosperity, defended our country, and preserved and protected the vision of our founding fathers. Through time, they have shared life's experiences and expertise, paving paths of progress, defining the foundation of which we continue to further the successes of today. They have built a legacy of excellence that will long endure.

I am certain that this expo will offer a wealth of lessons to our seniors, their adult children and caregivers, and others on financial literacy, health and best of all, "*How to live for tomorrow.*" I commend the *Mature Texan Magazine*, The Gallagher Group and AARP in your efforts and commitment to serve senior Texans. You highlight the best of the Lone Star State.

First Lady Anita Perry joins me in extending our best wishes for the future.

Sincerely,

Rick Perry

Rick Perry
Governor

The Flame:

But I tell you, love your enemies and pray for those that persecute you, that you may be children of your Father in heaven. He causes his sun to rise on the evil and the good, and sends rain on the righteous and the unrighteous.

Matthew 5:44–45

Now instead, you ought to forgive and comfort him, so that he will not be overwhelmed by excessive sorrow.

2 Corinthians 2:7

But if you do not forgive others their sins, your Father will not forgive your sins.

Matthew 6:15

FIRE IT UP!

This is who I need to forgive:

_____

_____

_____

_____

_____

_____

_____

_____

My Passionate Prayer Time:

_____

_____

_____

_____

_____

_____

_____

_____

33

Burning to Grow Money for You and Others

I love it, Lord, that your Word slams the reader with IN-YOUR-FACE principles about money:

DON'T LOVE IT.

Like the preacher said, "Never saw a U-Haul attached to a hearse."

May as well not love it because you're not ever going to keep it.

Own it? Great! Own all you want. Just don't let money own you.

Love it? Not so great because you'll marry it. And betrayal, divorce, and heartbreak are certain down the road.

For the love of money is a root of all kinds of evil. Some people, eager for money, have wandered from the faith and pierced themselves with many griefs.

1 Timothy 6:10

Lord, you have heard the flack I get from some viewers, listeners, and students when they hear me talk about:

- How to get double-digit returns safely
- How to cut, burn, and slash your taxes
- How to build a secure retirement
- How to accumulate college education funds for kids and grandkids
- How to leave an abundant, tax-free legacy

They think that's "love of money." And they say:

"Jesus did not talk like that!"

Yes, he did because he also said: "Love your neighbor."

Right?

Hey, that's not right. It's cut off somewhere.

You got it.

He said: "Love your neighbor AS YOURSELF."

We have a biblical, healthy, and urgent responsibility to take care of ourselves, I tell my audiences.

Your book, Lord, empowers us to take care of others as well. It's like the story of the flight attendant. We're up 25,000 feet in the air and she stands there and makes her announcements about the seatbelts, safety exits, and then says, "If we run into turbulence and there's an interruption in oxygen flow, yellow masks will drop from the bin above you. If you're with a minor child, then . . ." (What does she say?) She says: "Put your mask on FIRST. Then put the mask on the child."

We gotta take care of ourselves so we can take care of others.

Your book also says, "It's more blessed to give than to receive." Well, we can't give it unless we've got it.

> *Do not store up for yourselves treasures on earth, where moths and vermin destroy and where thieves break in and steal. But store up for yourselves treasures in heaven, where moths and vermin do not destroy and where thieves do not break in and steal. For where your treasure is, there your heart will be also.*
>
> Matthew 6:19–21

> *No one can serve two masters. Either you will hate the one and love the other, or you will be devoted to the one and despise the other. You cannot serve both God and money.*
>
> Matthew 6:24

> *. . . not given to drunkenness, not violent but gentle, not quarrelsome, not a lover of money.*
>
> 1 Timothy 3:3

Peter answered: "May your money perish with you, because you thought you could buy the gift of God with money!

Acts 8:20

Use it to take care of yourself and others. Sure enough, don't love it, but DO GIVE IT!

We give because GIVING IS YOUR GIFT TO US, right, Lord?

Here it is again, that great story on giving. The story was about Ranger, Texas, and the "oil boom that won the war." They were talking about World War I when oil erupted from the fields of West Texas like geysers at a water park.

And there was that tiny Bible church that discovered a global truth about you, Lord, and your laws of giving. They discovered oil there right there on the property. A nice, messy, spouting gusher. Conservatively, a petroleum engineer said they'd have $3,500 a month in royalties.

Instantly wealthy.

Then came Wednesday night meeting of the deacons, and they were preparing for Sunday's service. A young guy quipped, "We can leave the tithes and offering part of the service out. We don't need offerings anymore. Wooeee. We're going to be having about $3,500 a month coming in from them royalties."

L-O-T-S of money back then.

But Brother Ledbetter, the oldest and wisest among them, rose and says, "No, we'll still have the offering this Sunday and every Sunday. We'll still ask people to give for the widows, the orphans, the support of the church, for missions, for education, for the preacher, for benevolence. We'll still challenge them to give like we always do. We'll still have the offering: we give because we need to give. If we didn't give, we would dry up and die."

Give to the one who asks you and do not turn away from the one who wants to borrow from you.

Matthew 5:42

HOW TO EARN IT.

Thank You, Lord that your Word is bursting with these facts:

- "If a man does not care for his own household, he is worse than an infidel."
- "If a man does not work, neither shall he eat."
- "Whatever you sow, that you shall reap."
- "Look at the industrious ant."
- "Work unto the Lord."

I am burning to earn, Lord. I love the sweat, reward, and freedom of work.

I am burning to earn.

I'm like the fourteen-year-old boy burning to grab that summer courier job.

At 7:30 a.m. interviews began, said the paper.

At 7:00 a.m. he was there and he was boy number twenty-two in line. Seeing twenty-one boys in front of him, he snatched a square of paper from the curb, grabbed his pen, and scratched a note on the scrap. He ran to the secretary in front, plunged the note into her hand, and said, "Please give this to your boss immediately. It's urgent." The secretary looked, chuckled, and handed it to the boss.

"I am boy number twenty-two in line. Don't do anything until you see me."

He got the job.

He was burning to earn, and he loved to work.

Like John Wesley said four centuries ago: "Do all the good you can. By all the means you can. In all the ways you can. In all the places you can. At all the times you can. To all the people you can. As long as ever you can."

> *Anyone who has been stealing must steal no longer, but must work, doing something useful with his own hands, that they may have something to share with those in need.*
>
> Ephesians 4:28

> *For even when we were with you, we gave you this rule: "The one who is unwilling to work shall not eat."*
>
> 2 Thessalonians 3:10

HOW TO MAKE MONEY GROW

Lord, thank you for showing me the difference between black money, gray money, red money, blue money, and green money. You talked a lot about these colors in your story in Luke 19:12–26, didn't you?

> He said: "A man of noble birth went to a distant country to have himself appointed king and then to return.

> "So he called ten of his servants and gave them ten minas. 'Put this money to work,' he said, 'until I come back.'

> "But his subjects hated him and sent a delegation after him to say, 'We don't want this man to be our king.'

> "He was made king, however and returned home. Then he sent for the servants to whom he had given the money, in order to find out what they had gained with it.

> "The first one came and said, 'Sir, your mina has earned ten more.'

> "'Well done, my good servant!' his master replied. 'Because you have been trustworthy in a very small matter, take charge of ten cities.'

"*The second came and said, 'Sir, your mina has earned five more.'*

"*His master answered, 'You take charge of five cities.'*

"*Then another servant came and said, 'Sir, here is your mina; I have kept it laid away in a piece of cloth.'*

"'*I was afraid of you, because you are a hard man. You take out what you did not put in and reap what you did not sow.'*

"*His master replied, 'I will judge you by your own words, you wicked servant! You knew, did you, that I am a hard man, taking out what I did not put in and reaping what I did not sow?'*

"'*Why then didn't you put my money on deposit, so that when I came back, I could have collected it with interest?'*

"*Then he said to those standing by, 'Take his mina away from him and give it to the one who has ten minas.'*

"'Sir,' they said, 'he already has ten!'

"He replied, 'I tell you that to everyone who has, more will be given, but as for the one who has nothing, even what they have will be taken away.'"

Luke 19:12–26

Oh, I know you didn't use the color description that I do, but it's the same lesson.

Black money:

Dead. Money that does nothing, Money that is dead; money that is buried in the backyard.

Like the client who came telling me that he stuffed $20,000 cash in a moisture-proof box and buried it in the backyard. He didn't know someone saw him.

When he inspected his dig the next day, that money was gone. He ran to the bank asking the bank if they made a record of the serial numbers on the twenty-dollar bills.

Or the guy in Dallas, who called me to his home office and told me he was ready to complete the paperwork for his five-hundred-thousand-dollar rollover from Texas Instruments. I completed my questionnaire on due diligence and estate planning, and we completed the transfer paperwork on the rollover.

"Oh, one more thing, Dr. Gallagher. I've got $50,000 in cash."

"In a savings account? Or a safety deposit box?" I asked.

"No, I mean cash. Right there." And he jerked his thumb back over his shoulder to the wall and then scraped his chair across the Mexican tile and touched the place in the wall where the $50,000 lay stashed.

In cash.

"Want to count it?"

"Thanks, but no, thanks."

I didn't want to see it. I didn't want to know it was there. And I didn't want to tell him how unwise he had been with that money.

"Didn't you ever hear of a fire?" I questioned.

No response.

Or the lady who came to me with a million dollars in a checking account: A NON-INTEREST-BEARING CHECKING ACCOUNT. Dead money. Doing nothing. I say doing nothing, but it was doing a whole lot for the bank. It made the bank mighty happy.

Gray money:

Boring. Gray money is safe money, but some people confuse safe money with serious money, Lord. By serious money, I mean money that is growing above taxes and inflation and helping to build a secure retirement. Safe money is gray money, meaning that the principal will not go down. But it's not serious money. Serious money is money that takes into account the effects of taxes and inflation. And keeps the principal protected.

Safe money is CDs, savings accounts, money markets. They are short-term, liquid, and safe, but after taxes and inflation, folks end up with no growth and erosion of the money's buying power. And that's OK for some folks who want or need nothing but gray money.

Red money:

Alarm. Speculation. It's for those folks who can stomach the ups and downs of the stock market, precious metals, bonds, real estate, oil and gas. There's everything right in investing in the capital markets and helping to finance our free-enterprise system by being involved in the financial markets. But the problem is absolutely most people invest the wrong way. They invest unwisely:

- A hot tip
- An impulse
- I saw it on TV
- Got a recommendation from a friend
- I went to a seminar
- The broker's office is right down the street
- I got a cold call from a financial guy

None of these are good reasons, are they, Lord, to go ahead with a financial decision? I think it's smart to tell folks the facts about looking for a stock.

I tell them to look for seven signs:

- Earnings
- Innovation

- Dividend Yield
- Stock Splits
- Leadership
- Momentum
- Value Pricing

and then be patient. You may have to wait a long time, sometimes ten years or more before a stock, bond, mutual fund, variable annuity, real estate, or other variable investment rises again to its original level.

Brown money:

Decaying. Like the color of dirt or rust. The folks my radio colleague Dave Ramsey talks about. Debt. Debt, Debt, Debt. Sounds like death. Their net worth, peace of mind, quality of life is rotting. So instead of sucking it in and being happy to live on a limited budget and enjoying contentment, they want to outspend their neighbors and fellow workers and go deeper and deeper and deeper in debt.

Remember that "brown money" couple who came to me, Lord? Just thirty-five years old, $50,000 in credit card debt, debating suicide or divorce or both. We prayed them through that, walked them through that day by day, week by week, month by month and together, you and I, Lord, we got them out of that hole. We stopped the decay. We got them on a budget, convinced them to agree to help support each other. Not blame each other.

Blue money:

Hope. The color of the sky. A new day. The ideal investment. Some call it a hybrid annuity; others call it a fixed-index annuity. You know, Lord, I don't work for any of those companies, but I love this "ideal investment" because I have seen it give people superior returns while enjoying protection of principal. When the market is up, the client is up; when the market is down, the client is not down. Principal and profits are always protected.

I love to see folks enjoying the blue skies of blue money, those for whom it is suitable.

Finally, Green money:

Green Go. Go up higher than other investments while also enjoying safety of principal.

Life Settlements.

They've been around for a hundred years. By your grace and power, Lord, that magazine asked me to write the article on it. Here it is again:

THE COMPASSION STRATEGY
Double-Digit Returns to you, Double-Digit Relief for Others

Do you consider yourself to be a compassionate person?
Yes or No

Do you like to help other people?
Yes or No

If you could help a person and substantially help yourself, would that be of interest to you?

Yes or No

In helping this other person, would it also help you to earn double-digit returns on your money safely (no market risk)?

Yes or No

If your answer is YES, let me introduce you to "**Rancher Bill**."

Rancher Bill was a high-level engineer at Bell Helicopter. He earned a substantial salary and placed it into his 401k for twenty years. At the age of 45, he had a million dollars. One day, he said to his wife, "Honey, we are not getting any younger we have always wanted to own a ranch. Let's do it." They retired and purchased a ranch in West Texas. The next twenty years, he created a successful business in ranching. At the age of sixty-five, he and his wife retired from active ranching and began traveling, enjoying their grandchildren and family. At the age of eighty-two, Bill and his wife began to slow down and revisited their financial income. They wanted to enjoy their final years on the ranch sitting on the back porch watching the sun go down.

One day, Rancher Bill received a bill for $25K for a million-dollar life-insurance policy. He said to his wife, "You know, honey, we do not need to continue to keep this million-dollar policy. We have enough money; our house is paid off, and if something was to happen to me, you are taken care of. Why spend $25K a year? Besides, we can utilize the additional funds to purchase your prescription drugs, and I would like to take the kids on more trips and take more cruises, so let's not spend the $25K a year on something we do not need." Rancher Bill called the insurance company, and they said, "Well, Mr. Bill, there are two things you can do, you can stop paying on it, which would cancel the policy, or receive cash value." Rancher Bill said, "I've put $700,000 into it over the years, plus the earnings and you're saying just drop it, just let it go?" They responded with, "Well, yes sir, you can do that." Rancher Bill asked "Anything else? How much is the cash value?" The insurance company said, "$46,500." Rancher Bill almost fell to his oak wood floor. "That is it? After all of the money I put in?" asked Rancher Bill. "Well, yes, sir. But remember, Mr. Bill, as you get older, with this universal life-insurance policy that we explained to you in detail, the cost of insurance increases, so you have less to go into cash value over the years." Rancher Bill asked, "Is that all I can do?" The insurance company said, "Yes."

(This is a true story based on the customary practice of insurance companies. For decades companies have been telling people they only have two choices, drop it or receive cash value.)

Rancher Bill came to learn about a service called "life settlements" that appeared to be a third choice. He called a life settlement company and found out after several discussions the policy is considered an object he owns, just like property he owns, and he can sell the policy if he would like to. With the help of the life settlement group, he found someone who was willing to purchase his policy for $300,000 and they become the new owner. "Sounds good to me," said Rancher Bill. "This is a win-win. My doctors said I will be gone in five or six years, that is the reality of it; for me to get the $300,000 now looks like a buttered biscuit dripping with honey and dropping from heaven."

Rancher Bill found out that the buying and selling of life settlements has been practiced since 1911. In the era, Justice Oliver Wendell Holmes said, "A person can sell his life-insurance policy just like he can any other prized object." The reason why this information has not been shared with the public is because over the last several decades the larger banks and corporations have been buying life-settlement policies and have been earning between 10- to 15-percent return each year safely with no market risk. They have not divulged that information to the individual consumer. The insurance companies would rather have the consumer drop the policies and not have to pay out obligations later on. (Dirty little secret.)

It's the *Compassion Strategy.* Rancher Bill needs the money. It is very compassionate to buy the policy from him <u>because he needs the money</u>. That is why we call it the *Compassion Strategy*. A big buyer of life-settlement contracts is a man named Warren Buffet. Rule #1: Always protect your principal. Rule #2: See Rule #1. Buffett has been using life settlements to stabilize his other investments for decades.

Thank you, Lord, for showing me the colors of money and giving me discernment, patience, and compassion when showing these colors to clients and helping them choose what is best for them.

Thank you, thank you. Amen.

The Flame:

Do not store up for yourselves treasures on earth, where moths and vermin destroy and where thieves break in and steal. But store up for yourselves treasures in heaven, where moths and vermin do not destroy and where thieves do not break in and steal. For where your treasure is, there your heart will be also.

Matthew 6:19–21

FIRE IT UP!

This is how I burn for money to earn it, use it wisely, and teach others to use it wisely.

_____

_____

_____

_____

_____

_____

_____

_____

My Passionate Prayer Time:

_____

_____

_____

_____

_____

_____

_____

_____

34

Burning to Lift

By your grace and power, Lord, I'm going to make today a great day regardless of what other people Say,

> Think, or
>
> Do.

You showed me some time ago that I don't have the luxury of collapsing to self-pity. But that's another story.

I will make today a great day regardless of what other people say, think, or do. I will guard my words. I know that WORDS:

Lift or drag,

> Inspire or distress,
>
> > Infuse with the elixir of hope,
> >
> > > Or stab with a needle of cyanide.

And I know, Lord, the most important conversation I will have today (besides the one with you) is the one I have with myself. I know that Satan will try to stuff my skull with words like:

- You'll never get ahead.
- You're always making bad decisions.
- You should have gotten out of bed earlier.
- You shouldn't have talked to that person that way.
- You shouldn't have let them take advantage of you.
- You shouldn't have invested money in that area to begin with.
- You should have gone to school someplace else.
- You should have gotten a different job.
- You should have asked that person to help.
- You shouldn't have asked that person to help.
- You shouldn't have been late.
- You shouldn't have been early.
- And on and on.

The attacks of "shoulda, shoulda, shoulda" don't make sense.

I didn't plan those attacks, Lord, and I don't want them.

By your grace and power, I'm going to shove the "shouldas" in the toilet and flush. I will take what I've got and where I am and turn it into an instrument of your hope, courage, and victory.

I will remember what you said to Moses when he complained: "Lord, I should be better in speech. I should be better in leadership before I do your work."

And you said, "What is that in your hand?"

"A rod."

And you said, "Stop the shouldas, throw down the rod, and pick it up again in my power!"

Remind me, Lord, that it's never ability or inability, but it's AVAILABILITY that invites the honor of your appointment and the promise of your power.

Remind me, Lord, that I will hear thousands of words today: mall, market, office, gym, subway, radio, bus, and sidewalk. They'll talk about news flashes, bad traffic, soap operas, busted plans, and ugly problems. They'll talk, talk, talk, talk, and talk.

But will they lift? Lift themselves? Lift others? Will people rise when they hear these words? Will they grab solutions and work with energy and hope?

I hate to say it, Lord, but have you heard their words lately?

I ask, "How are you doing?"

The answer is, "You don't want to know." Or "Hey, it's Wednesday, we're over the hump."

"Could be worse."

"Not bad since it's payday."

"I'll make it—barely—but I'll make it."

"Life stinks. What else do you want to know?"

"That guy cut me off—what a jerk."

And the last one:

"I'm coping."

Coping? Why not CONQUERING?

By your grace and power, Lord, no matter what "they" say, I—ME, yes, me—I will make today a great day because TODAY IS YOUR GIFT TO ME. That's why it's called THE PRESENT. I arose before the sun today. Alive. I will rest after the sun sets today. Dead to the day. Resting. Resurrecting at dawn and getting ready to go again.

What did I do with that sixteen to eighteen hours of life today? What did I do between sunrise and sundown with my words? Did I live today like I was alive or like I was dead? Did I speak to others like they were alive or they were dead?

I know, Lord, I know—and you've heard them—they say, "You're naïve. There's so much famine, child abuse, worry, rape, poverty, crime, brutality, unfairness in the world."

"So," I ask, "how do we attack these heart-stabbing tragedies? With words of despair, complaint, or fatigue? They lead to surrender. No actions, no solutions."

Or do we attack with words of faith, hope, love, and courage, followed by sweat-busting work and human-rescuing ACTIONS?

I'm burning to lift today, Lord. Lift myself and lift others. I will remember that I will rise no higher than my words, and I can lift no one else higher than my words to them. And I'll make today a great day by my actions. I will visit the jails, nursing homes, and funeral parlors. I will take food to the hungry, shelter to the homeless, hope to the depressed, courage to the fearful, and friendship to the friendless. I will shake the hand of the shy, give money to the broke, and hug those who are untouchable. I will do the normal Christian life. Amen.

The Flame:

A bit in the mouth of a horse controls the whole horse. A small rudder on a huge ship in the hands of a skilled captain sets a course in the face of the strongest winds. A word out of your mouth may seem of no account, but it can accomplish nearly anything—or destroy it!

It only takes a spark, remember, to set off a forest fire. A careless or wrongly placed word out of your mouth can do that. By our speech we can ruin the world, turn harmony to chaos, throw mud on a reputation, send the whole world up in smoke and go up in smoke with it, smoke right from the pit of hell.

This is scary: You can tame a tiger, but you can't tame a tongue—it's never been done. The tongue runs wild, a wanton killer. With our tongues we bless God our Father; with the same tongues we curse the very men and women he made in his image. Curses and blessings out of the same mouth!

James 3:5–10 *The Message*

FIRE IT UP!

This is how I am burning to lift myself and others:

_____

_____

_____

_____

_____

_____

_____

_____

My Passionate Prayer Time:

_____

_____

_____

_____

_____

_____

_____

_____

35

Burning for Excellence in Work

Lord, in my work, remind me that my priorities begin with you:

- God
- Family
- Work

That's it.

Work is not my God, but

1. I work as though you were watching over my shoulder.

2. I work unto you and follow your principles of integrity and stewardship.

3. I owe my boss, my company 100 percent, maybe 110 percent.

4. I'm an employer, and I'm working for my employees 110 percent.

5. My work is my sacrifice of praise to you.

6. I will not complain about my work. If I have issues about my work, I talk openly to the people in charge.

7. I do not gossip at work.

8. I will remember that for some people, they stop working as soon as they get a job. That's not me.

9. I will have a passion for excellence about my work, seeking the best for all those around me, including my boss.

10. If I have employees, I do not regard them as people or instruments to be used and exploited for my profit. I see each of them as intrinsically valuable.

11. I praise my coworkers who are promoted. I do not submit to jealousy or sabotage.

12. I praise and encourage my employees for jobs well done. I honor them publicly.

Lord, thank you for the work you've given my hands to do. Amen.

The Flame:

For we are God's workmanship, created in Christ Jesus to do good works, which God prepared in advance for us to do.

Ephesians 2:10

Whatever you do, work at it with all your heart, as working for the Lord, not for men.

Colossians 3:23

FIRE IT UP!

This is how I work for my boss and serve my employees:

_____

_____

_____

_____

_____

_____

_____

_____

My Passionate Prayer Time:

_____

_____

_____

_____

_____

_____

_____

_____

_____

36

Burning to Repair Relationships Rapidly

God, I know Satan loves to rub a tiny abscess until it erupts into a foul, fatal infection.

I need your help, Lord. Drive me to repair relationships
> rapidly,
>> rapidly,
>>> rapidly.

The Three Rs: Repair Relationships Rapidly.

Satan's good at ripping relationships into shreds. At . . .
> church,
>> marriage,
>>> class,
>>>> company,
>>>>> team.

Impulsive glance.

Confusing body language.

Misunderstood words.

Tactless response.

"No big deal," we say.

"Fix it NOW," you say, Lord.

"Ahhh, leave it alone," Satan argues. "Let it rot a little longer. It can wait."

Too often, Lord, we ignore you and collapse to Satan.

So, another

church,

     marriage,

          class,

               company,

                    team

                         decays and dies.

You've seen it, Lord, and cried (as I have). Cousins, brothers, parents, children torn and bleeding for decades because someone

- lost his temper
- forgot to send a wedding invitation
- forgot a child's name
- couldn't make the birthday party
- got jealous over an inheritance
- was late for the graduation

"Get over it! Get on your knees!!" I can hear you saying, Lord.

Thank you, Lord. (While there's still time.) We can still

- lift the phone
- knock on the door

- bang out an e-mail
- say, "I was wrong. I am sorry."
- humble ourselves

"BUT I WASN'T WRONG!" I insist.

Doesn't matter—just find something good to do or say to the person who was wrong. One of those RAKS: Random Acts of Kindness. Everyone needs to give and receive RAKS because everyone makes mistakes—sometimes really stupid mistakes—and everyone needs healing.

Thank you, Lord, for saying it so simply: "Do well to those who hurt you."

And help me, Lord, to look in the mirror: "OK, when will you get smart enough, tough enough, loving enough, humble enough to be the one who steps forward to repair relationships?"

Thank you, Lord.

PS. Is it just me, Lord? Or does it strike you as a sad irony that FAMILY and CHURCH—where love, trust, and support should flourish—are often the places where relationships rot. Because no one repairs QUICKLY.

"Just the way I planned it!" cackles Satan.

The Flame:

Therefore confess your sins to each other and pray for each other so that you may be healed. The prayer of a righteous person is powerful and effective.

James 5:16

But I tell you, love your enemies and pray for those who persecute you.

Matthew 5:44

FIRE IT UP!

These are the relationships I need to repair rapidly:

_____

_____

_____

_____

_____

_____

_____

_____

My Passionate Prayer Time:

_____

_____

_____

_____

_____

_____

_____

_____

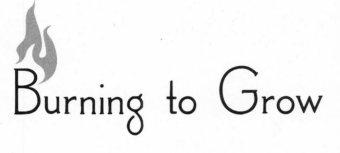

Burning to Grow

37

Burning to Smash the Five Ds

Lord, by your grace and power, I smash the five Ds. I better.

Because if the first one ever snatches me, the last one does too.

I get DISAPPOINTED, Lord.

Of course, I do.

In the poem "Andrea de Sorta," Robert Browning wrote, "Ah, a man's reach should exceed his grasp, / or what's a heaven for?"

You reach out to help so many people, don't you, Lord? You did it through your prophets and preachers for millennia. You certainly did it through Jesus and continue to do it through your Holy Spirit and your Church. So many people to help. So many opportunities. Surely at times, Lord, you have felt disappointment.

Me?

Lord, I surrender to sleep when I feel DISAPPOINTED. I reached so few, accomplished so little, and was smothered by so many problems,

> problems,

> > problems.

A real downer.

Spin my brain around, Lord, to rehearse what I <u>did accomplish</u> today and help me to journal what you and I will win tomorrow. When <u>I write</u> it, <u>I claim</u> it.

I know without your help, Lord, I'll slide from disappointment into DISCOURAGEMENT.

The devil was giving a tour of Hell to newly recruited demons.

"What's that Ferris wheel doing here?" a demon asked, pointing to the monstrous upright wheel, chains hanging and clanging from its sides.

"Not a Ferris wheel for sure," chuckled Satan. "No fun and games here. That's the body rack we supplied to European kings, a nice addition to their castle cellars. They squeezed the truth from spies, shot pain into enemies, and ripped bodies apart. Heh-heh-heh."

"And those posts? Charred, aren't they?" asked another demon. "Use them to light bonfires?"

"Yes." Satan's teeth gleamed. "Bonfires of bodies. Those are the Smithfield Pillars, a tribute to Bloody Mary's burning of heretics in 1555. Hundreds of them right in Market Square.

Crowds gasped as ears fell off and fingers sizzled."

"And that? Looks like a bouncy seat from one of those American water parks," another wide-eyed demon asked.

"No water games here. With this splashy seat," answered Satan, "we showed Chinese warlords how to strap dissidents into this seat and lower them into this tub. Full body. Scared the hell into them."

Thirty seconds under water.

Lift him up.

"You swear allegiance to Chou-Kan only?"

"Never."

Down he goes. One minute under water. And then a minute and a half. And then two minutes. He's getting the idea.

Up he comes.

"You swear allegiance to Chou-Kan only?"

"Never."

Down he goes.

Up, down, under.

Up, down, under.

Up, down, under.

Until the lungs vomit water and the throat gasps, "I swear allegiance to Chou-Kan only!"

"Must have been fun for you, Master S, to watch him fight for his life and watch the warlords laugh at his panic and fear."

"Spot on, kid! And the best part was when he shouted his allegiance to the watching crowd. (What a wimp he was to give up.) We dropped him in anyway. The warlords watched every bubble of life escape. We extracted the pain we wanted, warlords got the words they demanded, and the mob got the message."

Satan continued his fiery tour of the trophies of Lucifer:

Poison darts.

Iron garrets.

Gas chambers.

"Wha—, Wha—, What's that!?" asked the chorus of demons.

A rock the size of a man's fist sat in a trophy case, under lights, with the plaque "Lucifer's Best."

"See how the rock is beveled at the end to slip slowly into a man's soul? It's the rock of DISCOURAGEMENT. Our best weapon."

"Get that edge in a man, and we've got him. Forever on Earth, forever in Hell. He'll give up. He'll say, 'Telling the truth is stupid. Going to church is a waste. Helping other people is a joke. Being faithful to my family is a drag.'"

Protect me, Lord, today and every day. By your grace and power, help me recognize the pressure of that rock pushing into MY soul and replace it with the rock of Christ—my hope and my righteousness.

If not, you know what comes next. DESPONDENCY.

Now I really start to slide into "stinkin' thinkin."

Why should I try to live right?

So I skip church. Stop all Bible reading. Cut out my prayers. Lie a little here. Use people and begin

sinking,

sinking,

sinking

into DEPRESSION.

I shuffle. I drive like I'm in a fog. I don't eat at all (an early death wish), or I stuff myself to smother the DEPRESSION, only adding layers and layers of guilt and fat and more depression.

I sleep longer, pulling sheets over my head, shielding myself from sun and light that might bring hope.

There is no hope.

Getting close now, dangerously close to

DESPAIR.

I have seen it in others, Lord, and I feel ". . . the wretched man that I am" (as Paul said). If I didn't smash the DISAPPOINTMENT way back then when it started, it eventually does tumble into DESPAIR:

Disappointment

Discouragement

Despondency

Depression

Despair

With despair comes suicide.

The pit of no hope.

Suicide is the most selfish act ever because the tragedy leaves others feeling tormented, grieving, puzzled, and guilty.

"What did we do wrong?"

And suicide is the ultimate slap in the face to you, isn't it Lord? The guy (or girl) is saying, "There is no hope. There is no God." So, bam!

Take me back, Lord, to hope, to the fact that in Christ

my past has been forgiven,

my present is victorious, and

my future is secure.

Faith in those truths gives me power in the present.

Knock me off that first step of disappointment, Lord, reminding me of Mother Teresa's passion:

"I was not called to a ministry of success but one of <u>service</u>."

No disappointments there, just a burning to serve.

In all this you greatly rejoice, though now for a little while you may have had to suffer grief in all kinds of trials. These have come so that the proven genuineness of your faith—of greater worth than gold, which perishes even though refined by fire—may result in praise, glory and honor when Jesus Christ is revealed.

1 Peter 1:6–7

The Flame:

Praise be to the God and Father of our Lord Jesus Christ, the Father of compassion and the God of all comfort, who comforts us in all our troubles, so that we can comfort those in any trouble with the comfort we ourselves have received from God.

2 Corinthians 1:3–4

FIRE IT UP!

This is how I smash the 5 Ds:

_____

_____

_____

_____

_____

_____

_____

_____

My Passionate Prayer Time:

_____

_____

_____

_____

_____

_____

_____

_____

38

Burning to Say the Six Hardest Words

Lord, I've taught it to others. It's always hardest to teach it to myself. And it proves even harder to hear myself say it. "I WAS WRONG; I AM SORRY."

The six hardest words to express.

It's hard to get a cold fireplace blazing with wet wood and soggy matches.

It's just about as hard to ignite a cold heart to say: "I was wrong; I am sorry."

Remind me, Lord, to repair relationships quickly by saying those "six hardest" words.

Remind me, Lord, that absent these words, I trash my friendships and expose my hypocrisy.

Why is it so hard to speak these six words? I know it's healthy, Lord. I feel so good when I speak them.

So why is it so hard to speak these six words? Maybe it's because I'm like Eve from your Garden. I want to point the finger at someone else.

Now, JUST WHAT IF Eve had said to Adam and to you, Lord, "I was wrong; I am sorry"? Adam might have eschewed the apple, and we'd still be enjoying life in the garden.

Remind me, Lord, that "fessin' up" quickly helps in two ways: helps me heal and helps the other person heal too.

Just in from the Associated Press:

> The German manufacturer of Thalidomide, a drug that caused thousands of babies to be born with shortened arms and legs, or no limbs at all, issued ITS FIRST-EVER APOLOGY Friday—50 years after pulling the drug off the market.
>
> Gruenenthal Group's chief executive said the company wanted to apologize to mothers who took the drug during the 1950s and 1960s and to their children who suffered congenital birth defects.
>
> "We ask for forgiveness that for nearly 50 years we didn't find a way of reaching out to you from human being to human being," Harald Stock said. "We ask that you regard our long silence as a sign of the shock that your fate caused to us."

Stock spoke in the West German city of Stolberg, where the company is based, during the unveiling of a bronze statue symbolizing a child born without limbs.

The drug, given to pregnant women mostly to combat morning sickness, was pulled from the market in 1961. (Frank Jordans and Maria Cheng, "Maker of Thalidomide Apologizes," *Associated Press*, September 1, 2012.)

Don't wait fifty years.

Say the six hardest words now: I was wrong, I am sorry.

Then <u>do</u> whatever it takes to fix it.

The Flame:

Therefore confess your sins to each other and pray for each other so that you may be healed. The prayer of a righteous man is powerful and effective.

James 5:16

FIRE IT UP!

This is how I say the six hardest words:

_____

_____

_____

_____

_____

_____

_____

_____

My Passionate Prayer Time:

_____

_____

_____

_____

_____

_____

_____

_____

39

Burning to Choose

Lord, thank you for that jungle lesson when, whacking my way through the thick vines and tangled brush of northwest Thailand and rescuing villagers from isolation and despair, you taught me that THE JUNGLE IS NEUTRAL.

Many warned me not to go. The jungle, they said, was full of tigers, cobras, and poisonous plants. It was a green hell, and I would be dead within a few days. Could be.

But I learned that the jungle was also full of fresh fruit and cool water, right there for the eating and drinking. I learned to sleep standing up, sitting down, squatting. I learned I could bed in a tree safely. I learned that it was my state of mind, a state of mind that I chose, that determined whether the jungle was hostile to my survival or helpful to my mission of rescue. I learned that the jungle is neutral.

It was up to me to make it a perilous trek or a progressive adventure.

Just like my jungle of thoughts and moods.

Norman Vincent Peale wrote, "Change your thoughts and you change your world."

Thank you for the transition of the jungle to my daily life. With the gift of free will, I choose my thoughts. I choose my actions, and I help others to do the same.

It is the attitude, the state of mind, that determines the outcome of my day, for good or bad. It is MY state of mind that dumps me into a pit of failure or lifts me onto a platform of success. Thank you for teaching me that, Lord.

I choose my thoughts; I choose my actions.

The jungle of life, indeed, is neutral, and I choose whether to survive and succeed or to fret and ultimately fail. This day is neutral, and I choose to make it a great day regardless of what other people say, think, or do.

I choose my thoughts; I choose my actions. Amen.

The Flame:

But if serving the LORD seems undesirable to you, then choose for yourselves this day whom you will serve, whether the gods your forefathers served beyond the Euphrates, or the gods of the Amorites, in whose land you are living. But as for me and my household, we will serve the LORD.

Joshua 24:15

FIRE IT UP!

This is how I choose my thoughts, words, and actions today:

_____

_____

_____

_____

_____

_____

_____

_____

My Passionate Prayer Time:

_____

_____

_____

_____

_____

_____

_____

_____

40

Burning to Read

Lord, with your power, you could have flashed the Ten Commandments on photos on Facebook or Twitter or Instagram, so all the world could see them.

(You still could, Lord.)

You could have blasted the Ten Commandments from speakers the size of mountains so all could hear.

(You still could, Lord.)

To everybody. Everywhere.

But you had Moses etch your ten rules of love on a tablet for them and us to READ. And, millennia later, through your Son Jesus, you <u>wrote</u> in the sand for rock-throwers to read:

> *The teachers of the law and the Pharisees brought in a woman caught in adultery. They made her stand before the group and said to Jesus, "Teacher, this woman was caught in the act of adultery. In the Law*

Moses commanded us to stone such women. Now what do you say?" They were using this question as a trap, in order to have a basis for accusing him.

But Jesus bent down and started to write on the ground with his finger. When they kept on questioning him, he straightened up and said to them, "Let any one of you who is without sin be the first to throw a stone at her." Again he stooped down and wrote on the ground.

At this, those who heard began to go away one at a time, the older ones first, until only Jesus was left, with the woman still standing there. Jesus straightened up and asked her, "Woman, where are they? Has no one condemned you?"

"No one, sir," she said.

"Then neither do I condemn you," Jesus declared. "Go now and leave your life of sin."

John 8:3–11

By the way, Lord, what WAS it that Jesus wrote?
- "OK, which one of you guys set her up?"
- "This woman is a child of God, no matter what she's done."

- "Guys, are you trying to trap me?"
- "Hey, where's the dude she was doing the adultery with?"

Whatever he wrote, combined with his rebuke, it was enough to cause the accusers to drop their stones and leave the scene.

John <u>wrote</u>, "Jesus did many other things as well. If every one of them were written down, I suppose that even the whole world would not have room for the books that would be written" (John 21:25).

And decades after that, Paul said to his young apprentice Timothy: "Bring me the BOOKS I left in Troas" (2 Timothy 4:13).

He wanted them and us to have the joy of reading, whether it's

- a tablet,
- a book, or
- sand.

Read it!

What is it about this gray, spongy dome reigning under our skulls? Words love to race through its pulsating tunnels, sparking adventures in logic, order, reason, imagination, and finally, ah-hah! moments.

I am burning to read because I can do it over and over again. Slow or fast, mark it up, circle the best, paint it with notes.

Pass it on, and pass it down. Rewind it with my eyes and study it.

My librarian tells me only one in a thousand reads a book these days. The statistics on college grads are a little bit better. After people leave college, the average college grad reads one book a year. Maybe. God, help us. While the rest of the world gets

- seduced by TV fantasy,
- kidnapped by video games,
- drunk on Twitter bites, or
- addicted to Facebook gossip

shove my face, Lord, into a good book.

Beginning with yours.

Remind me, Lord, how a good book doesn't merely entertain—it's a mirror of my soul in which I see my fears and triumphs. It's a magnifying glass because I see magnified in its characters the virtues I embrace and the vices I eschew.

I love it, Lord, that as I read, time melts.

I forget about the white pages and black print. I weep, laugh, or rage with the heroes or heroines.

I love with them.

I am them.

Remind me, with good books, I

- climb Everest
- have tea with the queen
- change tires at the Indy Speedway
- haggle with diamond merchants in Antwerp
- fight dragons and villains (and win!)
- perform open-heart surgery

- embrace my son and daughter as I enjoy the feelings of other fathers embracing theirs.

Deliver me from the pack of thousands who ban books from their brains. And help me to be one who daily devours good books, nourishing my good brain, the gift you gave me.

Then the angel said to me, "Write this: Blessed are those who are invited to the wedding supper of the Lamb!" And he added, "These are the true words of God."

Revelation 19:9

The Flame:

When the LORD finished speaking to Moses on Mount Sinai, he gave him the two tablets of the covenant law, the tablets of stone inscribed by the finger of God.

Exodus 31:18

FIRE IT UP!

This is how I enrich my reading and feed my brain:

_____

_____

_____

_____

_____

_____

_____

My Passionate Prayer Time:

_____

_____

_____

_____

_____

_____

_____

_____

41

Burning to Control

Lord, help me to control my body, not let my body control me.
You know, Lord, how I love mounds of spaghetti floating
in marinara sauce, rich with the aroma of garlic and onions.
You know how I love the sting of wasabi racing through my
nose as I munch on sushi roll after sushi roll. You know how
I love the burn of jalapeños scorching my belly as I swallow
another five-alarm burrito dripping with green sauce and
steaming cheese.

And you know how I love to follow these feasts by gulping
a frothy, frigid strawberry shake.

Teach me control, Lord. I need your help. Yes, I know your
Word says that the Godly enjoy all things, and, yes, I know Jesus
said he came to give life and give it abundantly, and I know that
Jesus's first miracle was at a wedding feast in Cana.

Yes!

Thank you, Lord, that through Jesus you taught us that life is for laughin', lovin', and livin'.

I also know that your Word teaches that "people are slaves to whatever has mastered them" (2 Peter 2:19).

Beer, drugs, lasagna, banana splits, and cigarettes, whatever—deliver me from the possibility of ANY addiction that could compel me to gorge myself and lose control physically.

It's different for each of us guys, Lord; you know our individual points of weakness, and you're ready to infuse each of us with your Holy Spirit and deliverance. Thank you.

And, help me resist, Lord, when I am tempted to collapse into comparisons. Like the Pharisees, "God, I thank you that I am not like other men, robbers, evildoers, adulterers, even like this tax collector" (Luke 18:11–12).

I am tempted to criticize and judge: "Lord, I thank you that I am not a couch potato like other men, that I'm not grossly overweight; at least I run or pump three to four times a week, and I exercise some control over my eating. Thank you that I am not a TV slouch. Thank you that I am not like that." Help me NOT be a Pharisee like that, Lord.

Deliver me, Lord, from the comfort of comparison and the demon of denial.

I claim your power, Lord, and I announce my decision to embrace again the divine joy of fasting. To live one day a week without food, one week a month without it, and one month a year. I've done that before, Lord; I will do it again, as you lead me.

Remind me to take some of the time I would normally use to eat and to invest that time in eating and drinking in your Word and soaking in a spirit of prayer.

Food. I can't escape it. It's all around me. I can hide in excuses and gorge myself, or I can hide in the shelter of your grace and rejoice in our victories together. Amen.

The Flame:

The man without the Spirit does not accept the things that come from the Spirit of God, for they are foolishness to him and he cannot understand them, because they are spiritually discerned. The spiritual man makes judgments about ALL THINGS, but he himself is not subject to any man's judgment.

1 Corinthians 2:14–15

FIRE IT UP!

This is how I control my appetites:

_____

_____

_____

_____

_____

_____

_____

_____

My Passionate Prayer Time:

_____

_____

_____

_____

_____

_____

_____

_____

_____

42

Burning to Run

Lord, you know I love the comfort of the sheets caressing me in the morning. Blast me out of bed and kick me out the door to run, to walk, to do some form of physical exercise.

I know the two forces: pleasure and pain.

Just the thought of the pain is the force that kills the run before it starts. I wince at the thought of hitting that runner's wall.

Right from the start, I'll grab for air with my lungs feeling as heavy as bricks and slam my feet on the ground with my legs feeling as stiff as steel. My quads will shout, "Stop!" My heart will scream for rest. My arms will refuse to rise and swing.

But I know the pleasure. I know that after busting through the pain I will feel the warm endorphins flooding my arteries, igniting a glow of euphoria. I will feel hot sweat bubbling from my pores, purging my body of its toxins and waste.

The pain or the pleasure.

"The difference between successful people and unsuccessful people is simply this. Unsuccessful people don't do the things that they don't like to do. **Successful people DO the things that they don't like to do.**" Zig Ziglar said that.

Thanks again, Zig.

Lord, your man doesn't wait to "feel" his way into a better way of acting, does he? Your man ACTS his way to a better way of feeling. Plant deep in my subconscious that feeling of the swish-swish of flesh sliding against flesh as I feel my armpits lubricate. Back and forth, back and forth, like pistons sloshing through oil and propelling my body forward. Stamp on the front of my brain a bright neon reminder: "It feels so good."

Thank you that I have heels that can hit the pavement and I can roll forward along the balls of my feet. Thank you for a big toe on each foot to press into the pavement and push me forward. Thank you that I have knees to cushion the jolt and quads to support my weight and keep me balanced and upright.

Slow or fast. Cold or hot. Short or long. Thank you that I can run. Or walk or swim. Thank you, Lord, that I am fearfully and wonderfully made. Amen.

The Flame:

Do you not know that your bodies are temples of the Holy Spirit, who is in you, whom you have received from God? You are not your own; you were bought at a price. Therefore honor God with your bodies.

1 Corinthians 6:19–20

FIRE IT UP!

This is how I commit to physical exercise:

_____

_____

_____

_____

_____

_____

_____

_____

My Passionate Prayer Time:

_____

_____

_____

_____

_____

_____

_____

_____

43

Burning to Seek and Save the Lost

Lord, my desire is to follow Jesus's command: seek and save the lost and to make disciples of all nations.

Whether I feel like it or not.

Beginning right here, right now. Gym, office, factory, playground, or neighborhood. Right here, right now, because I desire it. I desire it because you have honored me and other Christians with the great commission.

> *"Therefore go and make disciples of all nations, baptizing them in the name of the Father and of the Son and of the Holy Spirit, and teaching them to obey everything I have commanded you. And surely I am with you always, to the very end of the age."*
>
> Matthew 28:19–20

Remind me, Lord, to be patient with those Christians who say they feel no obligation or compassion to seek and save the lost, nor to make disciples. They don't know DESIRE.

DESIRE IS FIRE.

You know the story, Lord, of the man walking home from work one night, cold and dark. He decided to escape the cold, so he took a shortcut across the small cemetery in the middle of town. Little did he know earlier that day a grave had been dug but not filled in.

You remember what happened: he stumbled into the six-foot grave, black, cold, quiet. He screamed: "Help! Get me out of here. Help, help, help." Louder and louder.

Nobody. A black, cold night, and nobody heard his desperate cry. He grabbed the slimy walls, only to pull out thin roots and muddy chunks. He shoved his toes into the soft walls to get a footing, and his foot slipped as fast as he stepped. After one hour, when the sweat inside his clothes exceeded the sweat dripping from his face, he hunkered down in one corner of his dark tomb, guarding whatever warmth he could until morning came.

But he heard the sound of someone walking! Before he could rise to speak, the inevitable happened. Man number two stumbled into the other side of the grave. Man number two screamed, "Help! Help! Help! Someone get me out of here." Man number two jumped and climbed; he shoved his feet into the slimy wall, also to no avail. In pity, man number one from the far side of the grave cupped his hands around his mouth and said, "You can't get out of here."

But he did.

A fictitious story, but a factual passion.

DESIRE IS FIRE.

Here's a true one:

> Several years ago, a large eagle in Scotland snatched from the front of a small cottage a sleeping baby wrapped in light clothing. Several people witnessed the event, and quickly the whole village turned out, trying to catch the eagle as it flew away with the baby. However, eagles fly and people don't, so the eagle landed on a lofty crag. Most of the people from the village lost all hope for the child's life. However, some of the villagers were determined to exhaust every possible avenue and make the effort to save the baby before conceding what appeared to be the inevitable.
>
> First, a sailor who was between trips tried to climb to the high nest. But after a time he reached an impasse, accepted defeat, and abandoned the effort. He had failed, but others refused to quit. Next, a rugged, experienced highlander who was accustomed to mountain

climbing also tried. Although he got closer to the baby, he too could not quite make it, so he turned back in failure.

A frail peasant woman stood silently by while all of this was going on. Then she indicated that she was going to try. No one said anything, but it was obvious that everyone was thinking if a healthy young sailor and a rugged highlander had failed to scale the heights, what chance did this frail woman have? She removed her shoes and started putting her bare feet first on one shelf of the cliff, then another, and another until she rose to the level of the child. She lifted the baby from the eagle's nest while the villagers waiting below watched anxiously and fearfully.

The descent was even more difficult than the climb because one wrong step would now result in the death of two people. Carrying the infant added to the difficulty. But slowly, step-by-step, the woman descended the side of the mountain. Once she hit the bottom, the amazed villagers welcomed her. She was able to succeed while others failed because she had a different kind of motivation. She was the mother, and the desire to rescue the baby was the fire that ignited the climb.

Remind me, Lord, how millions have been snatched by Satan, and they are now trapped in a nest of deceit. They need me (and other Christians) to rescue them.

Remind me, Lord, that millions are still living in cold, dark graves awaiting me and other Christians to teach them, love them, and lead them into the warmth and light of your love.

Help me to see people as you see them, Lord: trapped and scared. Give me your desire to seek and save the lost. Cause me to light on fire with passion to burn, to seek, and to save the lost. Amen.

The Flame:

For the Son of Man came to seek and to save the lost.

Luke 19:10

Therefore go and make disciples of all nations, baptizing them in the name of the Father and of the Son and of the Holy Spirit, and teaching them to obey everything I have commanded you. And surely I am with you always, to the very end of the age.

Matthew 28:19–20

FIRE IT UP!

This is how I will seek and save the lost:

_____

_____

_____

_____

_____

_____

_____

My Passionate Prayer Time:

_____

_____

_____

_____

_____

_____

_____

44

Burning to be Grateful

Lord, thank you for showing me today in my quiet time that a grateful person is a great person; a grateful person is a happy person.

Jesus said to the leper who was healed and returned: "Where are the nine? Where are the other nine who were healed?"

Lord, by your grace and power, I will not be one of the nine who left ungrateful. I will be the one who says, "Thank you."

Lord, I read those studies that document that a grateful person

- is more optimistic,
- exercises more,
- thinks more creatively,
- bounces back from adversity faster,
- is less intimidated by challenges,
- has a higher immune response,

- is more alert and interested,
- is more adventurous,
- is likely to live longer,
- is more likely to help others,
- is more likeable,
- is more tolerant,
- is a better boss or team leader,
- is a better employee, student, or child, and
- has a zest for life that keeps him and others cheering and winning even in times of pain and failure.

Lord, thank you for the gift of gratitude. Amen.

The Flame:

Rejoice always, pray continually, give thanks in all circumstances; for this is God's will for you in Christ Jesus.

1 Thessalonians 5:16–18

FIRE IT UP!

This is how I will show gratitude today:

_____

_____

_____

_____

_____

_____

_____

_____

My Passionate Prayer Time:

_____

_____

_____

_____

_____

_____

_____

45

Burning to Dream

How do you drive people crazy?
Stop their dreaming!

Lord, I read those studies where psychologists took a select group of subjects and hooked up their sleeping heads to machines that tell when they were deep in sleep and when they started to dream. When the subjects started to dream, the psychologists woke them up, and then let them go back to sleep.

Each time the subjects went back to sleep and started dreaming, they were awakened again. Even though each night the subjects received enough hours of sleep, that was not the problem. After one night of this type of treatment, some of the subjects were nervous and fidgety. After a second night, many were irritable and cross, despite the fact that they were still enjoying an appropriate amount of sleep. At the end of three nights of getting the same amount of sleep with NO dreaming, the researchers ended the experiment because some of the subjects were showing severe psychological stress. They were going crazy!

Twenty-four hours later, after normal sleep (with dreaming), the subjects were back to normal. The experiment showed that when you sleep, YOU MUST HAVE DREAMS.

And when you're awake, you must have dreams too.

- A dream
- A goal
- A passion
- A vision

Thank you for telling us in your Word, Lord:

Where there is no vision, the people perish.

Proverbs 29:18

No vision, no dreams, no passion.

Help me, Lord, to keep posted in front of me the phrase you showed me years ago:

"What would I do with my life if money were no object? What would I do with my life if I were independently wealthy?"

Answering that question empowers me to see the dream, goal, vision, and passion that you gave me.

And help me, Lord, to ignite in others the gift of pursuing a dream. The problem is that many are afraid to dream. So much of the input they've received has been negative. They've been told all their lives what they CAN'T do instead of what they

CAN do. Sadly, so many people don't know what they want because they don't know what's available to them, which is especially tragic in America where opportunities remain virtually unlimited.

Not realizing the treasure we have in America, many people still get up and go to work today because that's what they did yesterday. Work to them is just a habit. The job is a necessary but unfulfilling paycheck. Life is boring. They drift from one job, from one city to another.

No vision, no dreams, no passion. They are dead long before they get dumped in the ground.

In short, they float like debris from shipwrecks. They're not "full-steam-ahead" captains steering the ship of purpose and progress.

Burning to dream, Lord. I'm burning to dream for me and for you. And I'm burning to help others to dream. Amen.

The Flame:

Where there is no vision, the people perish.

Proverbs 29:18

FIRE IT UP!

This is how I will dream and help others to dream:

_____

_____

_____

_____

_____

_____

_____

My Passionate Prayer Time:

_____

_____

_____

_____

_____

_____

_____

_____

46

Burning to Repent

L ord, thank you for your optimistic truth.

> *In the same way, I tell you, there is rejoicing in*
> *the presence of the angels of God over one sinner*
> *who repents.*
>
> Luke 15:10

Lord, I want to be real. Help me to repent. Show me what needs to be purged from my life.

I'm burning to repent. Not just saying, "I'm sorry," but ACTING in ways that show I repent. I know that behavior betrays belief and action dramatizes truth.

Years ago, a London newspaper ran a contest saying, "What's wrong with the world? The person who sends in the best essay will be our winner."

G. K. Chesterson's entry won. His essay was entitled simply "I am."

Chesterson recognized, as few people do, the prophet Jeremiah's truth: "The human heart is desperately wicked. Who can understand it?" There is a powerful, snarling force in every human that can easily be fed and later unleashed in evil acts. Cruel. Demonic. Barbarous. There's the potential for an angel in all of us, and there's also the potential for abject evil.

That's why I want to repent quickly, Lord, to avoid the possibility of Satan taking over.

Pray, Seek, Turn, Repent. That works, Lord.

It begins with me, doesn't it, Lord?

I reject the cliché: "Well, that's just the way I am."

And I reject the flippant cliché: "The devil made me do it." No!

I have free will. I can be transformed by you.

I repent. I resist sin. I rebuke Satan. I change.

I'm burning to repent and be purged and made clean to be a stronger man for your service. Amen.

The Flame:

Peter replied, "Repent and be baptized, every one of you, in the name of Jesus Christ for the forgiveness of your sins. And you will receive the gift of the Holy Spirit.

Acts 2:38

"Even if they sin against you seven times in a day and seven times come back to you saying 'I repent,' you must forgive them."

Luke 17:4

FIRE IT UP!

These are some attitudes, actions, and thoughts of which I repent:

_____

_____

_____

_____

_____

_____

_____

My Passionate Prayer Time:

_____

_____

_____

_____

_____

_____

_____

47

Burning to Banish Fear

Lord, I love your saying: "Perfect love casts out fear."
It cuts to the chase, doesn't it? Fear:

False

Evidence

Appearing

Real

What is this false evidence? It's the lie in my skull. "I can't do this. I can't handle it. It'll smother me. I'll never get over it." Instead, by your grace and power, Lord, I will repeat: "I can do all things through Christ, who strengthens me" (Philippians 4:13).

Whatever it is, I'll say in advance, "I'll handle it."

I will remember that your love blasts fear. I'll believe in your glorious guarantee: "Perfect love drives out fear."

I can do all things through Christ, who strengthens me. I believe you, Lord.

Like the old saying says, "Ships are safe in the harbor, but that's not what ships are made for."

I will remember that on this sea of life I am on a journey to grow and improve and to rescue others. I will remember that there are high seas and frightening storms, but I will not stay in the harbor of fear.

I will grow and improve and take reasonable chances to exercise what you have given me. I'll banish fear by remembering that "all things work together for good for those who are called by God according to His purpose."

I will say "Yes" to whatever happens. I will not collapse into a victim's state of mind, saying, "Oh, why did this happen to me? That's not fair."

I will not be a victim. I will say, "Yes." I will say, "It is what it is," and make something good out of it.

Yes. I'm burning to banish fear by saying "Yes" and by repeating, "I can do all things through Christ, who strengthens me." Praise your glorious name, Lord. Amen.

The Flame:

In God, whose word I praise—in God I trust and am not afraid. What can mere mortals do to me?

Psalm 56:4

I can do all this through him who gives me strength.

Philippians 4:13

And we know that in all things God works for the good of those who love him, who have been called according to his purpose.

Romans 8:28

FIRE IT UP!

This is how I banish fear:

_____

_____

_____

_____

_____

_____

_____

_____

My Passionate Prayer Time:

_____

_____

_____

_____

_____

_____

_____

_____

48

Burning to Fast

Restore my love of fasting, Lord, because you and I know that:

(1) Fasting disciplines.

After supper. "More potatoes, sweetie?"

"Yes, OK and while you're in there, put some more of that g-o-o-o-d gravy on it." (I have to have seconds—makes my wife feel good. Right?)

8:45 p.m. "Want some ice cream?"

"Sounds like a winner. Thanks." (She'll have a bowl probably, and people don't like to eat alone.)

Along with the ice cream, I plunge my fist in a vanilla wafer box. Can't eat ice cream by itself! Followed by a handful of nuts or a glass of milk. (So a sweet taste won't stay in my mouth. Right?)

Once I start slamming fistfuls of crunch in my mouth, I keep going. And I find excuses to deceive myself.

Fasting slaps me. It reminds me that food is primarily for fuel, not fun. Oh, I know, Lord, Paul said that everything is to be enjoyed, so I'm not talking about laying down rigid rules for me or others. I'm just reminding myself that, well, food is primarily for fuel. If I forget that, then the fun becomes gluttony.

(2) Fasting trims.

Thank you, Lord, for reminding me of your victories through me in fasting. Thank you for reminding me that my body is a divine building, a home for your Holy Spirit. Fasting teaches me to be an alert manager. When I fast, I find myself running, stretching, lifting more. I breathe heavier and deeper. I'm not going to wait, Lord, until I'm old and obese before I decide to trim this temple.

(3) Fasting frees up funds and food.

Fasting frees up funds and food to feed the hungry. By fasting, Lord, you've shown me that I can save what? Ten dollars a day, which I then dedicate to famine-fighting ministries. Fasting for this reason also has an explosive, expansive effect. I don't do it for show, but I do know other people catch the commitment and do likewise.

Ask Mother Teresa:

"Excuse me," Mother Teresa said. "How much does this meal cost?"

The flight attendant shrugged. "I don't know. About one dollar in US currency."

"If I give it back to you, would you give me that dollar to give to the poor?"

The flight attendant looked startled. "I don't know if I can," she stammered. "It's not something we normally do." The flight attendant left her cart and went to the front of the plane to consult with the pilot. A few minutes later, she returned. "Yes, Mother," she said, "you may have the money for the poor."

"Here you are." Mother Teresa handed her the tray. The couple in front did the same. The attendant started down the aisle. Suddenly it seemed no one on that flight wanted to eat lunch. The flight attendant got on the speaker and said: "If anyone wants to give up their meal, the airline will give one dollar to Mother Teresa for the poor."

None of the 129 people on that flight, including the crew, wanted lunch. At the end, $129 was set aside for the poor.

The plane landed and Mother Teresa wasn't done. She asked the airline officials on the tarmac for the 129 trays and for a truck and a driver.

"You throw the food away anyway. Take me to the poorest part of your city."

She handed out 129 meals to shanty dwellers.

Fasting. Amazing what it will do to inspire the overfed to feed the underfed. Oh and Lord, thank you for reminding me that when I fast, it takes my mind off my own problems. What a gift.

(4) <u>Fasting frees me to count my blessings</u>.

It was a long time ago, Lord, but you and I remember those days when I shuffled to grade school hungry. I floated into the school cafeteria hungry, smelling molasses-coated baked beans and warm, rising yeast rolls and butterscotch brownies. I deliberately sat alone at a table, head aching and staring at a book, pretending I was so absorbed that I didn't care about eating. And I remember shuffling home again hungry.

Now I can eat anytime I want and as much as I want. I am on top of one-tenth of one percent of the prosperous in the world. Warren Buffett said he was grateful that he won the ovarian lottery, meaning that he was born at that time and at that place where he had more chances than anyone else in the world.

Me too. Me three.

Fasting—feeling hunger, real hunger—frees me to count my blessings.

(5) <u>Fasting smacks Satan</u>.

Lord, you have shown me that the practice of fasting cripples Satan's attacks on me. Remind me, Lord, that you did give Satan temporary reign over the earth and its material parts, one of which is my body. Remember Job?

> *Be alert and of sober mind. Your enemy the devil prowls around like a roaring lion looking for someone to devour.*
>
> 1 Peter 5:8

My body is flesh and game for Satan. I discover the more I deny my appetites, the more I deny Satan access to my body. Whether that's lusting for sex, power, or food.

For me, thank you, Lord, I've learned twenty-one meals a week are relentless. Such a constant pattern of stuffing hardly disciplines my body for work and service. Fasting (for me) punches Satan between his lips, knocks out his teeth, and drives him away from this body.

Remind me, Lord, that my fasting brings grace and freedom. I do not fast to earn your favor. I do not collapse into the pagan practices of damaging my body to earn heaven, or purifying my spirit, or winning the rewards of karma.

No way.

I fast because I want to. I fast because it is a gift from you.

I'm burning to fast, Lord. Burning to improve body, mind, and spirit for you. Amen.

The Flame:

When you fast, do not look somber as the hypo-crites do, for they disfigure their faces to show others they are fasting. Truly I tell you, they have received their reward in full.

Matthew 6:16

However, this kind does not go out except by prayer and fasting.

Matthew 17:21

FIRE IT UP!

This is how I fast:

_____

_____

_____

_____

_____

_____

_____

_____

My Passionate Prayer Time:

_____

_____

_____

_____

_____

_____

_____

_____

49

Burning to Live

Every day is a gift from you, Lord. Isn't that why we call it THE PRESENT?

I've heard it a thousand times and I embrace it, Lord.

I will live with

> Exuberance,
>
> Excitement, and
>
> Joy.

And remind me, Lord, that the world does not owe me a pain-free existence or guarantee me comfort. Lord, I'm glad you made me an emotional being who can feel disappointment as well as exuberance, sadness as well as excitement, and pain as well as joy. Rescue me, Lord, from the naïve and foolish belief that the positive emotions of exuberance, excitement, and joy are somehow my birthright, a constitutional right. Remind me that with the adventure of these positive emotions inevitably comes the attack of negative ones.

Thank you, Lord, that the negative ones remind me that I am created in your likeness and I am alive. I can recognize the negatives, respond to them, and turn them into positives.

Thank you, Lord, for showing me that it's naïve and dangerous for me to think that there is such a thing as a pain-free life.

And remind me, Lord, that the more I reach out

- to risk,
- to grow, and
- to serve others,

the more I'll get whacked.

So what's the alternative? Whining and worrying all the time? Teddy Roosevelt summed it up nicely:

> The credit belongs to the man who is actually in the arena; whose face is marred by sweat and blood; who strives valiantly; who errs and comes short again and again because there is no effort without error and shortcoming; who knows the great enthusiasms, the great devotion, spends himself in a worthy cause; who at best knows in the end the triumph of high achievement; and who at worst, if he fails, at least fails while daring greatly, so that his place shall never be with those cold and timid souls who have never tasted victory or defeat.

I want to live, Lord. Really live.

I will not be a cold and timid soul. By your grace and power, I will GRATEFULLY taste the sweetness of victory and the bitterness of defeat all the days of my life.

victory and defeat

victory and defeat

victory and defeat

Bring 'em on

Thank you, Lord.

"The only easy day was yesterday," the Navy Seals say. They got it right.

The Flame:

I have come that they may have life and have it to the full.

John 10:10

This is what I have observed to be good: that it is appropriate for a person to eat, to drink, and to find satisfaction in their toilsome labor under the sun during the few days of life God has given them—for this is their lot. Moreover, when God gives someone wealth and possessions, and the ability to enjoy them, to accept their lot and be happy in their toil—this is a gift of God.

Ecclesiastes 5:18–19

FIRE IT UP!

This is how I live with exuberance:

_____

_____

_____

_____

_____

_____

_____

My Passionate Prayer Time:

_____

_____

_____

_____

_____

_____

_____

50

Burning to Act

God, what's wrong with this GPS?
I set it right, Lord.

It shows me how to get from 301 Mitchell Street in Ft. Worth to 1005 Mockingbird Lane in Dallas. This GPS even talks to me and tells me (a) how far it is, (b) when to turn, and (c) the approximate arrival time.

What's wrong? GPS is right, isn't it?

Oh.

I forgot to put the key in?

Of course.   Key in,

                    Crank it,

                    Slam it into gear,

                    Mash pedal,

                    Drive.

Five acts.

GPS is useless without ignition and motion.

Thanks for reminding me of your byte: the only thing that counts is faith WORKING through love (Galatians 5:6).

By your grace and power, I act. I do the loving thing, the right thing. Now.

Good to dream. Good to plan. Good to know. Good to talk. Best to act.

Move. Fire it up. Act. Faith without action is dead. You said that, Lord.

By your grace and power, I act. I use the logs of planning, dreaming, and studying to stoke the flames of action and, again, I keep Zig's truth posted in front of me:

"The only difference between a successful person and an unsuccessful person is this: Unsuccessful people don't do the things they don't want to do. Successful people DO the things that they don't want to do."

Blast me out of my lethargy. I embrace the battle Paul talked about in Romans:

> *"I do not understand what I do. For what I want to do, I do not do."*
>
> Romans 7:15

I KNOW what I want to do to strengthen the ties of my family. I KNOW what I want to do to improve my business and better serve clients. I KNOW what I want to do to fortify my body and purify my mind. I KNOW what I want to do to challenge, comfort, and inspire others.

By your grace and power, I do it. I act now. I do the right thing whether I feel like it or not. I act now.

I join with Jeremiah when he said, "There is fire in my bones because of your spirit of fire in me."

> But if I say, "I will not mention his word or speak any more in his name," his word is in my heart like a fire, a fire shut up in my bones. I am weary of holding it in; indeed, I cannot.
>
> Jeremiah 20:9

I will say to fear, delay, and procrastination, "Get thee behind me." I will conquer fear by doing the thing I fear and by claiming your truth that "perfect love casts out fear."

Because I love you, Lord, and because I love people, I will act. This is the time, this is the place, and I am your man. By your grace and power, I act.

For I know that to be a man means:

Delay I kill with duty, doubt I smother with faith, fear I purge with action. My dreams are dust, my speeches are scraps, and my faith is dead without action.

> Then I said to them, "You see the trouble we are in: Jerusalem lies in ruins and its gates have been burned with fire. Come, let us rebuild the wall of Jerusalem and we will no longer be in disgrace."

I also told them about the gracious hand of my God upon me and what the king had said to me.

They replied, "Let us start rebuilding." So they began this good work.

Nehemiah 2:17–18

The Flame:

Then the righteous will answer him, 'Lord, when did we see you hungry and feed you, or thirsty and give you something to drink? When did we see you a stranger and invite you in, or needing clothes and clothe you? When did we see you sick or in prison and go to visit you?'

The King will reply, 'Truly I tell you, whatever you did for one of the least of these brothers of mine, you did for me.'

Matthew 25:37–40

FIRE IT UP!

This is how I act:

_____

_____

_____

_____

_____

_____

_____

My Passionate Prayer Time:

_____

_____

_____

_____

_____

_____

_____

51

Burning to Learn

Lord, thank you for Frank Sullivan.
Sixty-second lesson, lifetime legacy.

Frank reminded me that everyone's my teacher when I:

- Ask
- Listen
- Apply

Yes, I know that it's necessary to sift the good from the bad, the strong from the weak, the truth from the fake, but I will first listen,

> and learn,

> > and discern,

> > > by your grace and power.

It was nearly fifty years ago, wasn't it, Lord? I was making my rounds as a medic. I hadn't seen Sullivan for a week. I prepped him for surgery that previous Friday. It was back on my weekend shift after a week in classes. I knocked on his door and walked in carrying a thermometer and BP cuff. Ready for vitals.

"Mr. Sullivan, how are you doing? Glad to see you. How'd the surgery go? How are we doing?" I chirped.

"Top of the morning, Neil," he said, dropping dollops of words in his Irish brogue, as smooth and mellow as honey. "Let me tell you, lad," he said, pushing his palms on each side of his hips and hoisting himself up, his gown flapping around his shoulders, "if you can sit up in bed, throw your legs around, stand up, and sip a cup of coffee, you're in good shape. Magnificent shape, saints be praised."

Right on.

Millions of guys can't sit up. They're paralyzed. Millions can't stand up. No legs. Millions can't sip coffee. No hands to lift a cup, no lips to sip.

Thank you, Lord. I can sit, stand, and sip.

Thank you, Lord. I asked, I listened, I learned.

And, Lord, remember the time as a young adventurer following my Peace Corps service, trekking around the globe with my thumb? Hitchhiking on the Autobahn, I caught the attention of a steel-gray Mercedes. It slid to a halt. Driver rolled down the window: "Welkom."

I jumped in, dumped my backpack in the back seat, belted in, and he quickly shot to 93 mph. His name was Hans, and he looked like Kirk Douglas. He sported waves of butterscotch-blond hair flowing to the back of his head. Fingers as thick as cigars gripped the lustrous, tan wheel. His fingernails were jagged like tiny mountain peaks. His fingers were scarred, and his knuckles were crooked. His chiseled chin snapped up and down as he answered my questions, speaking in halting English.

"What do you do?" I asked. "How's life in Germany?"

He told his story of the Berlin Wall.

He dug under it. Fingers were his pick and shovel. Like a mole, he tunneled. Caught. Brilliant physicist.

"We need him. We can't kill him."

Back to the lab under tight security. Sedated his captors. Flees in the night. Digs again, ripping his fingers to bloody stubs of flesh.

Escapes.

Freedom.

Wow! What a lesson, Lord. Thank you. With money challenges, family needs, business barriers, and so much to do with so little time, at least I know **I am free**.

I learned much from Hans, and I cherish my freedom.

And deliver me, God, from thinking that all I can learn is within my small skull or my small circle. Help me to see people as you see them. Each person is a bundle of experiences, victories, lessons, insights. Doesn't have to be a Governor Mike Huckabee, Nolan Ryan, Joel Osteen, Dr. Charles Stanley, Dr. Ken Cooper, or others I've interviewed over the years. Lots of lessons with them for sure, but I remember the story Dr. Dobson told of the fourteen-year-old boy.

Semi got jammed under a bridge. What to do? Engineers called in. File down the roof of the semi? Blast rock from the base of the bridge?

How do we get under there to file the semi or blast the rock?

Paperboy biking down the sidewalk saw the problem, heard the anguish, and said, "Why don't you guys just let the air out of the tires?"

Thank you, Lord, that you give insight and intuition to all. Squash my pride, shatter my ego, and open my eyes and mind to learn from everyone and anyone. Thank you, Lord. Amen.

The Flame:

For everything that was written in the past was written to teach us, so that through the endurance taught in Scriptures and the encouragement they provide we might have hope.

Romans 15:4

You will know the truth, and the truth will set you free.

John 8:32

FIRE IT UP!!

This is how I learn from everyone and anyone:

_____

_____

_____

_____

_____

_____

_____

_____

My Passionate Prayer Time:

_____

_____

_____

_____

_____

_____

_____

_____

52

Burning to Journal

Lord, I want to write it. Help me to slow down and write it. When I write it, I see it, and I get it.

"Write on," I hear you saying.

What is it, Lord, about taking pen in hand and stabbing paper with cursive letters like I'm doing now? Or etching them on a computer screen through keyboard keys? What is it that delivers that clarity, direction, and power?

Perhaps it's because I don't keep problems glued in my head anymore, do I? It's like looking at a map, a map drawn by me and for me. Now I can SEE where I'm going. It's like a blueprint for a house. I can see how the pieces fit. Help me to write it truthfully, Lord, and daily, so I can see where I've been and see where I'm going.

You know, Lord, sometimes my brain is a storm of fears, hopes, and feelings. My pen serves as a lightning rod taking those fears, hopes, and feelings and channeling them to explode on paper. When I write, I order the storm cloud to shoot its energy through my shoulder, elbow, wrist, hand, and fingers onto paper.

Onto <u>this</u> paper. Onto this screen.

And there I see the problem and write the solutions by your grace and power. Help me, Lord, to write it. Daily. Thank you. Amen.

The Flame:

Write, therefore, what you have seen, what is now and what will take place later.

Revelation 1:19

FIRE IT UP!

This is how I journal:

_____

_____

_____

_____

_____

_____

_____

_____

My Passionate Prayer Time:

_____

_____

_____

_____

_____

_____

_____

_____

53

Burning to Live the "Big Six"

Lord, by your grace and power, I will

- FORGIVE like it is my last day on earth
- LOVE like I've never been hurt
- WORK like I don't need the money
- DANCE like no one is watching
- SING like no one's listening
- LIVE with exuberance and joy.

I will remember that life is for laughing, loving, and living. It's not for whining, working, and worrying. (OK, I know we have to work but if we love what we do, then it's not work is it, Lord?)

Life is for laughing, loving, and living.

Thank you for reminding us of this, Lord, when you said

The thief comes only to steal and kill and destroy;
I have come that they may have life, and have it
to the full.

John 10:10

And, by your grace and power, Lord, I will remember that:

NO ONE KNOWS ENOUGH TO WORRY.
No one knows enough to worry because we do not know the future. We cannot predict the future, but Ta-da! WE DO CREATE IT BY OUR MOMENT-TO-MOMENT POSITIVE ACTIONS, WHETHER WE FEEL LIKE IT OR NOT.

Thank you, Lord.

The Flame:

The thief comes only to steal and kill and destroy;
I have come that they may have life, and have it
to the full.

John 10:10

FIRE IT UP!

Here's how I will claim your power to be bigger than my problems:

_____

_____

_____

_____

_____

_____

_____

_____

My Passionate Prayer Time:

_____

_____

_____

_____

_____

_____

_____

_____

54

Burning to Laugh

Lord, the doctors got it! Maybe they were reading Proverbs 17:22. Perhaps this prompted those physicians at the University of California to see if the therapy of laughter could be verified. Sure enough, it was.

Their controlled studies documented the benefits of laughter:

- Pain relief,
- Mood improvement,
- Lower blood pressure,
- Reduction in stress,
- Increase in muscle relaxation,
- Decrease in anxieties and fears, and
- A boost in the immune system.

And their colleagues in the psychology department confirmed it. Embracing humor in tough times helps men and women to

- Normalize the experience and
- Keep things from appearing too overwhelming.

Humor, they discovered, also is a powerful aid to

- Finding solutions,
- Making progress, and
- Helping men and women jump out of the pit of depression.

Humor, the physicians and psychologists added, also provides more energy throughout the day.

Every day.

In the University of Maryland study, (did you see it, Lord?), researchers studied a controlled group watching two types of movies: those watching an intense drama, and those watching a light comedy. Those watching the intense drama felt depressed and their blood flow decreased by about 35 percent. Those watching the comedy felt elated, and their blood flows INCREASED by 22 percent, vastly improving their heart rates.

Researchers concluded that **laughter may be as healthy as exercise and sex**.

Thank you, Lord, for the gift of laughter. I'm burning to laugh at myself and my problems, opening myself up to the therapy, relaxation, and solutions that you have prepared for me.

Lord, I'm burning to laugh because your Word says it's good, it's really good. Amen.

The Flame:

A cheerful heart is good medicine, but a crushed spirit dries up the bones.

Proverbs 17:22

A happy heart makes the face cheerful, but heartache crushes the spirit.

Proverbs 15:13

All the days of the oppressed are wretched, but the cheerful heart has a continual feast.

Proverbs 15:15

FIRE IT UP!

This is how I will laugh today:

_____

_____

_____

_____

_____

_____

_____

_____

_____

My Passionate Prayer Time:

_____

_____

_____

_____

_____

_____

_____

_____

_____

_____

55

Burning to be Bigger Than My Problems

Thank you, Lord, that because of your grace and power, I am bigger than my problems.

Talk-show heads want me to scream mantras of self-esteem or shout affirmations of determination. But it's by your grace and power that I am bigger than my problems. Thank you.

You are the source of my self-esteem and my daily determination. You are my provider.

And thank you for reminding me, Lord, of that portrait of Daniel in the lions' den. The portrait shows the placid Daniel looking up while he is stroking the head of a now-docile lion. Daniel's hands are on the head of the lion, but Daniel's head is lifted up toward you.

It's a word picture that a thousand preachers have proclaimed in a thousand sermons. Daniel wasn't looking down at the lions—he was looking up at you. That's what made him calm and courageous.

He burned with a holy fire to be bigger than his problems.

Thank you, Lord. Amen.

The Flame:

For it is God who works in you to will and to act in order to fulfill his good purpose.

Philippians 2:13

I can do all this through him who gives me strength.

Philippians 4:13

FIRE IT UP!

Here's how I will claim your power to be bigger than my problems:

_____

_____

_____

_____

_____

_____

_____

_____

My Passionate Prayer Time:

_____

_____

_____

_____

_____

_____

_____

_____

56

Burning to Plant

Lord, restore me to your garden—the one you intended for men and women originally. The fruits are still there for those who plant your seeds of love, joy, peace, patience, kindness, goodness, faithfulness, and self-control.

> *But the fruit of the Spirit is love, joy, peace, forbearance, kindness, goodness, faithfulness, gentleness and self-control.*
>
> Galatians 5:22

Adam and Eve had it all and blew it. You planted it for them and handed it to them—Your garden of unconditional love. They chose to let Satan plant seeds of doubt, worry, and pride.

To live *your* life, Lord, of purity and power, peace and purpose remind me TODAY to plant only seeds that are pure, positive, and powerful.

And remind me of your invincible law of planting and growing:

- thoughts are the seeds that nourish beliefs,
- beliefs erupt into actions,
- actions change to habits,
- habits switch to character,
- character transforms to destiny, and
- destiny is life.

Unlike Adam and Eve, who chose Satan as the master of their thoughts, I choose you. By your grace and power, I know that obstacles are what I see when I take my eyes off my goals. Your goals for me.

I will train and discipline my thoughts, allowing external circumstances to erupt into present opportunities for progress. I will not react to circumstances. I am a man, and in response to circumstances, I will act with your power principle:

IN EVERY ADVERSITY, THERE IS THE SEED OF AN EQUAL OR GREATER OPPORTUNITY.

When I plant that thought, I will see grand opportunities, not obstacles. Thank you.

Remind me, Lord, that if I don't plant your seeds of truth, purity, and power daily, then seeds of waste, decay, and despair will grow in me, rotting my soul. When others say, "It doesn't make any difference what you see or hear," help me to fight it like I would fight a serial killer hacking at my door.

I know my subconscious hears all and absorbs all. I will fight to make sure that I feed my subconscious only the pure, positive, and powerful.

I will repeat to myself and to my children the old Indian tale:

One evening a Cherokee chief told his grandson about a battle that goes on inside people. He said, "My son, the battle is between two wolves inside us all.

"One is evil—it is anger, envy, jealousy, sorrow, regret, greed, arrogance, self-pity, guilt, resentment, inferiority, lies, false pride, superiority, and ego.

"The other is good—it is joy, peace, love, hope, serenity, humility, kindness, benevolence, empathy, generosity, truth, compassion, and faith."

The grandson thought about it for a minute and then asked his grandfather: "Which wolf wins?"

"The one you feed," the chief replied.

Remind me that whatever I attract into my life, that's what I become. Remind me that circumstances do not make the man, but they reveal the man to himself. Remind me that when I think like a man of God and act like a man of God, I will attract circumstances and people who strengthen me and allow me to strengthen them.

Thank you, Lord, that in your majestic plan, I can plant my thoughts. I do not let the culture or the media plant thoughts in me or for me. I plants thoughts of <u>purity</u>, <u>power</u>, and <u>purpose</u> (PPP).

And I cultivate a life that glorifies you, while using the gifts and talents you've given me, Lord. Amen.

The Flame:

Finally, brothers and sisters, whatever is true, whatever is noble, whatever is right, whatever is pure, whatever is lovely, whatever is admirable— if anything is excellent or praiseworthy—think about such things.

Philippians 4:8

FIRE IT UP!

This is how I plant PPP in my mind:

_____

_____

_____

_____

_____

_____

_____

My Passionate Prayer Time:

_____

_____

_____

_____

_____

_____

_____

_____

57

Burning to be Patient

Lord, remind me that anger is a raw feeling, boiling in the belly of a person who feels wronged about something. And the anger is often ignited by bad facts and fueled by hot revenge. In dealing with anger, Lord, I will never be a skunk that just sprays over everything:

"Tell 'em what you think! Let 'em have it!"

Nor will I be a turtle and just hide:

"Stuff it in. Don't say a word."

Give me the grace to say, "Look, I need to report my feelings," and then help me to place my hand on the other person's shoulder and report my feelings without attacking or accusing. Or, make a conciliatory call. Or, write a letter of openness and appreciation.

By your grace and power, I will ACT with patience to identify and resolve the roots of my anger.

First, help me to be careful who I hang around with because impatient, hot-headed people will smash me if I embrace their example. They're infectious.

> *Do not make friends with a hot-tempered person,*
> *do not associate with one easily angered.*
>
> Proverbs 22:24

Second, I'll surrender my worries and anxieties to you knowing that worry often erupts into anger. And I will ask, "What would Jesus do?" I will then listen for your answer.

Third, in dealing with my anger and impatience, Lord, remind me to get some rest. I know my emotions are fragile when I'm fatigued.

Fourth, I will change expectations. Why do I sometimes get angry with the people around me? It's because I have expectations of them that may be unfair and unrealistic or that I've not made plain. Help me to have expectations that are balanced and true and to communicate them often and effectively.

Fifth, Lord, I will take a long run or a long walk when I start to feel heated emotionally. I will let the anger flow from my body in hot sweat or heavy breathing. Then I can deliver solutions in a cool and productive way.

I will remember, Lord, that in my anger and impatience, I often say things I don't mean and do things I normally wouldn't do. Rescue me from those dual tragedies.

Do not be anxious about anything, but in every situation, by prayer and petition, with thanksgiving, present your requests to God.

Philippians 4:6

"In your anger do not sin": Do not let the sun go down while you are still angry, and do not give the devil a foothold.

Ephesians 4:26–27

The Flame:

Better a patient person than a warrior, one with self-control than one who takes a city.

Proverbs 16:32

FIRE IT UP!

This is how I will be patient:

_____

_____

_____

_____

_____

_____

_____

_____

My Passionate Prayer Time:

_____

_____

_____

_____

_____

_____

_____

58

Burning to Make Today a Great Day

Lord, I will make today a great day, regardless of what *other* people say, think, or do.

Because your Word—and our promise—says so.

THIS IS the day that the Lord has made. I will rejoice and be glad in it, declares the Psalmist.

It does <u>not</u> say: This COULD be the day

- If I get a job
- If my husband remembers to call me during the day
- If my coworker across the partition stops her complaining
- If my kids turn down the music
- If the plumber shows up when he's supposed to.

This day is a gift to me. That's why it's called "The Present." And what a gift it is!

I've had about 21,000 of these gifts so far. 21,000 days I've been alive.

And hope to have another 21,000.

(OK, Lord, to be realistic, maybe another 9,000.)

I'll remember that the Psalmist doesn't say,

- "I will regret today."
- "I will endure today."
- "I will suffer through today."

He says, "I will <u>rejoice</u> in it."

And I will rejoice in today because

- I can breathe
- I can feel
- I can choose
- I can love, giving it, receiving it.

I am not a rock, tree, lizard, or weed.

I am alive in Christ, fashioned in the image of an

> All-loving,
>
> All powerful,
>
> All knowing,
>
> > Creator God.

And I will rejoice in it because this is another day that I enjoy life and help others enjoy life.

That's the whipped cream on top of the sundae. And the sundae is this day.

This is the day I REALLY get it:

I am made in YOUR image (Genesis 1:27).

You said it.

I believe it.

That settles it.

And what is that image, Lord, if it isn't strength, power, purity, and love?

You said it.

I believe it.

That settles it. Amen.

The Flame:

The Lord has done it this very day; let us rejoice today and be glad.

Psalm 118:24

FIRE IT UP!

This is how I will make today a great day:

_____

_____

_____

_____

_____

_____

_____

_____

My Passionate Prayer Time:

_____

_____

_____

_____

_____

_____

_____

_____

Burning for America

Burning for My Nation

Lord, I lift up America to you with all of her sin and rebellion. Continue to have mercy and patience and don't dump on us the full consequences of what we have sown by our silence.

Lord, I've got my nose on the floor and my hands spread out pleading for your forgiveness in letting this Christian nation slip into "USA." Pundits say it stands for United States of Atheism. No it doesn't—it stands for United States of Anarchy. We are a wild, undisciplined, pleasure-saturated bunch addicted to lust, titillation, and instant, explosive gratification.

Lord, you made it very clear in Psalm 33:12.

> *Blessed is the nation whose God is the Lord, the*
> *people he chose for his inheritance.*
>
> Psalm 33:12

You also said,

If my people, who are called by my name, will humble themselves and pray and seek my face and turn from their wicked ways, then I will hear from heaven, and I will forgive their sin and will heal their land.

2 Chronicles 7:14

How dangerously far we have come from being the Christian nation that you anointed.

Thank you, Lord, for the men and women you used to build this country as a Christian nation.

Our Presidents:

GEORGE WASHINGTON:

"It is the duty of all nations to acknowledge the providence of Almighty God, to obey His will, to be grateful for His benefits, and humbly to implore His protection and favor."

JOHN ADAMS:

"We have no government armed with power capable of contending with human passions unbridled by morality and religion. **Our Constitution was made only for a moral and religious people.** It is wholly inadequate to the government of any other."

THOMAS JEFFERSON:

"And can the liberties of a nation be thought secure when we have removed their only firm basis, a conviction in the minds of the people that these liberties are of a gift of God? That they are not to be violated but with His wrath? Indeed I tremble for my country when I reflect that God is just; that His justice cannot sleep forever."

JOHN QUINCY ADAMS:

"Is it not that in the chain of human events, the birthday of the nation is indissolubly linked with the birthday of the Savior? That it forms a leading event in the progress of the Gospel dispensation? Is it not that the Declaration of Independence first organized the social compact on the foundation of the Redeemer's mission upon earth? That it laid the cornerstone of human government upon the first precepts of Christianity?"

ABRAHAM LINCOLN:

"In regards to this great book (the Bible), I have but to say it is the best gift God has given to man. All the good the Savior gave to the world was communicated through this book. But for it we could not know right from wrong. All things most desirable for man's welfare, here and hereafter, are found portrayed in it."

THEODORE ROOSEVELT:

"I believe that the next half century will determine if we will advance the cause of Christian civilization or revert to the horrors of brutal paganism."

CALVIN COOLIDGE:

"The foundations of our society and our government rest so much on the teachings of the Bible that it would be difficult to support them if faith in these teachings would cease to be practically universal in our country."

FRANKLIN ROOSEVELT:

"The United States is founded on the principles of Christianity."

HARRY TRUMAN:

"The fundamental basis of this Nation's law was given to Moses on the Mount. The fundamental basis of our Bill of Rights comes from the teachings which we get from Exodus and St. Matthew, from Isaiah and St. Paul.

"This Nation was established by men who believed in God . . . You will see the evidence of this deep religious faith on every hand.

"This is a Christian nation."

DWIGHT D. EISENHOWER:

"Without God there could be no American form of government, nor an American way of life. Recognition of the Supreme Being is the first, the most basic expression of Americanism. Thus, the founding fathers of America saw it, and thus with God's help, it will continue to be."

JOHN F. KENNEDY:

"For I have sworn before you, the American people, and Almighty God the solemn oath our forebears prescribed.

"And yet the same revolutionary beliefs for which our forebears fought are still at issue around the globe—the belief that the rights of man come not from the generosity of the state, but from the hand of God."

RONALD REAGAN:

"For centuries the Bible's emphasis on compassion and love for our neighbor has inspired institutional and governmental expressions of benevolent outreach such as private charity, the establishment of schools and hospitals, and the abolition of slavery.

"The Congress of the United States, in recognition of the unique contribution of the Bible in shaping the history and character of this nation, and so many of its citizens, has by Senate Joint Resolution 165 authorized and requested the president to designate the year 1983 as the 'Year of the Bible.'

"Inside the Bible's pages lie the answers to all the problems that mankind has ever known. I hope Americans will read and study the Bible."

GEORGE W. BUSH:

"When you turn your heart and life over to Christ, when you accept Christ as the Savior, it changes your heart. It changes your life. And that's what happened to me.

"I believe that God has planted in every human heart the desire to live in freedom. And even when that desire is crushed by tyranny for decades, it will rise again.

"But I'm mindful in a free society that people can worship if they want to or not. You're equally an American if you choose to worship an Almighty and if you choose not to. If you're a Christian, Jew, or Muslim, you're equally an American. That's the great thing about America is the right to worship the way you see fit. Prayer and religion sustain me. I receive calmness in the storms of the presidency. I love the fact that people pray for me and my family all around the country. Somebody asked me one time, how do you know? I said I just feel it.

"We need common-sense judges who understand our rights were derived from God.

"May He guide us. And may God continue to bless the United States of America."

In addition to our presidents, other leaders affirmed our Christian heritage and identity:

PATRICK HENRY:

"An appeal to arms and to the God of hosts is all that is left us! Sir, we are not weak if we make a proper use of those means which God hath placed in our power. . . . Besides, sir, we shall not fight our battles alone. There is a just God who presides over the destinies of nations and who will raise up friends to fight our battles for us. . . . Is life so dear, or peace so sweet as to be purchased at the price of chains and slavery? Forbid it, Almighty God! I know not what course others may take; but as for me, give me liberty or give me death!"

JEDEDIAH MORSE:

"To the kindly influence of Christianity we owe that degree of civil freedom, and political and social happiness, which mankind now enjoys. . . . Whenever the pillars of Christianity shall be overthrown, our present republican form of government—and all blessings which flow from them—must fall with them."

BENJAMIN FRANKLIN:

"I've lived, sir, a long time, and the longer I live, the more convincing proofs I see of this truth: That God governs in the affairs of men. If a sparrow cannot fall to the ground without His notice, is it probable that an empire can rise without His aid? We've been assured in the sacred writings that unless the Lord builds the house, they labor in vain to build it. I firmly believe this, and I also believe that without His concurring aid, we shall succeed in this political building no better than the builders of Babel."

In the early days of America, the most famous and accurate observer of the American experience was Alexis de Tocqueville. In *Democracy in America*, he wrote:

> "The Americans combine the notions of Christianity and of liberty so intimately in their minds that it is impossible to make them conceive the one without the other. Upon my arrival in the United States, the religious aspect of the country was the first thing that struck my attention; and the longer I stayed there, the more did I perceive the great political consequences resulting from this state of things, to which I was unaccustomed. In France I had almost always seen the spirit of religion and the spirit of freedom pursuing courses diametrically opposed to each other; but in America I found that they were intimately united, and that they reigned in common over the same country."

De Tocqueville's countryman Achille Murat observed:

> "There is no country in which the people are as religious as in the United States. . . . The great number of religious societies existing in the

United States is truly surprising: there are some of them for everything; for instance, societies to distribute the Bible; to distribute tracts; to encourage religious journals; to convert, civilize, educate . . . to take care of their widows and orphans; to preach, extend, purify, preserve, reform the faith; to build chapels, endow congregations, support seminaries . . . to establish Sunday schools . . . to prevent drunkenness."

In early America, our Ivy League universities were the lighthouses in education (they should be today) for all generations in America. Founded as godly and prestigious institutions, Brown University (my alma mater) had deep Baptist roots; Princeton, Presbyterian; Harvard, Congregationalist; and Yale, Methodist.

Harvard and Yale stated their commissions and dedications in their student handbooks:

HARVARD:

"Let every student be plainly instructed and earnestly pressed to consider well the main end of his life and studies is to know God and Jesus Christ which is eternal life (John 17:3) and therefore to lay Christ as the only foundation of all sound knowledge and learning. And seeing

the Lord only giveth wisdom, let everyone seriously set himself by prayer in secret to seek it of
Him (Proverbs 2, 3). Every one shall so exercise
himself in reading the Scriptures twice a day
that he shall be ready to give such an account of
his proficiency therein" (Harvard 1636 Student
Guidelines).

YALE:

"All the scholars are required to live a religious
and blameless life according to the rules of God's
Word, diligently reading the Holy Scriptures,
that fountain of Divine light and truth, and
constantly attending all the duties of religion"
(Yale 1787 Student Guidelines).

With that kind of heritage, the world came to recognize
America as a Christian nation. That is the very reason the ex-
tremist Islamic world hates America—because they definitely
perceive her as a Christian nation and therefore, an infidel
nation, a tool of Satan, in their view.

The original and authoritative Supreme Court justices verified that this is a Christian nation, and other justices throughout
United States history affirmed the same.

For openers, (1) as you enter the Supreme Court courtroom, the two huge doors have the Ten Commandments engraved on them and (2) the Ten Commandments are also engraved over the chair of the Chief Justice.

JUSTICE JOHN JAY:

"The Bible is the best of all books, for it is the word of God and teaches us the way to be happy in this world and in the next. Continue therefore to read it and to regulate your life by its precepts.

"Providence has given to our people the choice of their rulers, and it is the duty, as well as the privilege and interest of our Christian nation, to select and prefer Christians for their rulers."

JUSTICE JAMES WILSON:

"Human law must rest its authority ultimately upon the authority of that law which is Divine. . . . Far from being rivals or enemies, religion and law are twin sisters, friends, and mutual assistants. Indeed, these two sciences run into each other."

JUSTICE JOSEPH STORY:

"One of the beautiful boasts of our municipal jurisprudence is that Christianity is a part of the Common Law. . . . There never has been a period in which the Common Law did not recognize Christianity as lying at its foundations. . . . I verily believe Christianity necessary to the support of civil society."

Following up on the Supreme Court's recognition of the United States as a Christian nation, there was the celebrated case of the *Church of the Holy Trinity v. United States* in 1892 in which the court promulgated a unanimous decision to coin America as a Christian nation. The US Supreme Court in that decision cited dozens of court rulings and legal documents as precedent to arrive at the ruling.

In the *Church of the Holy Trinity v. United States* decision, the court said:

> "There is no dissonance in these [legal] declarations. . . . These are not individual sayings, declarations of private persons: they are organic [legal, governmental] utterances; they speak the voice of the entire people. . . . These, and many other matters which might be noticed, add a volume of unofficial declarations to the mass of organic utterances that this is a Christian nation."

Following up on the Christian basis for America, the court case called *Vidal v. Girard's Executors* promulgated the following decision:

"Why may not the Bible, and especially the New Testament, without note or comment, be read and taught as a divine revelation in [schools]—its general precepts expounded, its evidences explained and its principles of morality inculcated? . . . Where can the purest principles of morality be learned so clearly or as perfectly as from the New Testament?" (1844).

Thank you, Lord, for America's Christian foundation which you laid by our forbearers. Amen.

The Flame:

Blessed is the nation whose God is the Lord, the people he chose for his inheritance.

Psalm 33:12

FIRE IT UP!

This is how I honor the United States as a Christian nation and a nation under God and how I work to restore its biblical heritage:

_____

_____

_____

_____

_____

_____

_____

My Passionate Prayer Time:

_____

_____

_____

_____

_____

_____

_____

60

Burning to Celebrate America's Uniqueness

America is different from other nations, isn't she, Lord?

1. Unlike all other nations past or present, this one accepted as a self-evident and divine truth that all men are created equal. Wow. That smashed world history. What this meant was that its founders created a society in which, for the first time in the history of the world, the individual's fate would NOT be determined by who his father was but by his own origin as a created human being, and one whose destiny is freely chosen by pursuit of his own ambitions.

Wow again!

America was something new under the sun, a society in which hereditary status and class distinctions were erased, leaving individuals free to act and to be judged ON THEIR OWN MERITS ALONE.

2. In all other countries, membership or citizenship was a matter of birth or blood or lineage or heredity. Thus, foreigners who were admitted for one reason or another into that country could never become full-fledged and successful members of that society. But in America, no such factors came into play. To become a full-fledged American, it was only necessary to pledge allegiance to the new republic and to the principles for which it stood, both moral and legal.

3. In all other nations, the rights, if any, enjoyed by their citizens were conferred—often arbitrarily—by human agencies, kings and princes, and occasionally parliaments. As such, these fragile rights amounted to privileges that could be revoked at will by the same human agencies. In America, by contrast, the citizen's rights—OUR rights—were declared from the beginning to have come from God and to be "inalienable"—that is, immune to legitimate revocation.

I've read the stats and the odds, Lord. One in thirty-six. No lottery, no Las Vegas player, would ever take those odds, but you bestowed them on me, Lord, and I won.

I am unique in the world.

I had a one in thirty-six chance of being born in America—land of the free, home of the brave, and the best prepared ground ever for education, progress, and success.

Thank you. Thank you. Thank you, Lord.

I praise you, Lord, for this gift, and I celebrate America's uniqueness. Amen.

The Flame:

Give thanks in all circumstances; for this is God's will for you in Christ Jesus.

1 Thessalonians 5:18

FIRE IT UP!

This is how I express my gratitude for living in America:

_____

_____

_____

_____

_____

_____

_____

_____

My Passionate Prayer Time:

_____

_____

_____

_____

_____

_____

_____

_____

61

Burning to Write the News Right

You write it right, Lord. They don't.

BMB (Big Media Boys) select the events that pander to a BMB worldview, mix it with mud and slime, call them "facts," and dump them on the public as sewage, which they call "news."

Not you, Lord. You tell it straight. Facts, Cause, Action, Consequence, Solutions.

Example: Your news report on David and Bathsheba.

First, here's how the BMB would have reported it:

Just in: King David had an affair with Bathsheba, the wife of army general Uriah. King David put a contract out on Uriah and had him killed. After that, David and Bathsheba had a child and the child died. Over to you, Sid. What's the weather look like this weekend?"

"Stuff happens," BMB shrugs, and then they drop it.

Here's how you would have reported it, in the popular press, (actually, you DID summarize the event this way in your Book):

<u>Facts</u>: David saw Bathsheba and collapsed into temptation. Bathsheba wasn't too swift and bathed naked on the roof next to David's palace. (Maybe she wanted to seduce him? Or somebody?)

<u>Cause</u>: Laziness or stupidity on Bathsheba's part, lust on David's.

<u>Action</u>: Adultery, lies, betrayal, murder.

<u>Consequence</u>: David got caught. Anguish. Grief. Guilt. Pain to one's self. Pain to others. Death of a child.

<u>Godly Solutions</u>: Repent. God forgives you. Now, forgive yourself. Get married, start a family, and start all over again.

Lord, it's no wonder my fellow Americans go to bed depressed and angry, and, the very next day, wake up sluggish and despairing. They still feel the slime of "news" stuck on their brains and a flood of problems drowning their souls.

There's no truth in the "news," no solutions, and most certainly, no hope.

Lord, when I have to be subjected to the news, remind me to grab a pen and write the news the way you have written it. The real facts: Cause, Action, Consequence, and Godly Solutions.

PS. I noticed, Lord, in your Book, you didn't call it an "affair," "tryst," "dalliance," or "making love." You nailed it: adultery. And adultery brings bad consequences. (Here in Dallas, you remember that guy, Lord, who got blown away <u>in bed</u> by his gun-toting wife, who caught him.) Now, those are the facts (brutal as they are), and that's the news the way it should be reported.

Sin has consequences. Sin also has solutions (God's way). Neither the consequences nor the solutions are reported by the mainstream media.

But they should be.

"The public has the right to know," they blather.

The public also has a right and a need to hear the whole truth and to be given Godly solutions and Godly hope. Lord, help me to stand in the gap and write the news your way. Amen.

The Flame:

Do not be deceived: God cannot be mocked. A man reaps what he sows.

Galatians 6:7

FIRE IT UP!

This is how I write the news your way, Lord:

_____

_____

_____

_____

_____

_____

_____

My Passionate Prayer Time:

_____

_____

_____

_____

_____

_____

_____

_____

62

Burning "To Be or Not To Be?"

Is that the question today, Lord, or is it "TV or not TV"?

I prefer the latter question because that's the life-threatening issue.

I remember, Lord, the father you sent to me for counseling for matters related to dealing with his dazed son.

The boy's mother abandoned the family. His father left the boy at home to watch TV. All day. Kid was drugged, dazed, and delirious. His eyeballs jumped like the flickering images of a television screen. He couldn't finish a sentence. Couldn't focus his eyes on me.

"The doctor says there's nothing wrong with him physically. Just watches too much TV. Huh. What do you think, Dr. Gallagher?" the father asked.

One look at the kid and I knew the doctor was right. The kid's mind was mud, his speech was slush, and his body slumped like Jell-O pudding.

I remembered reading, Lord, in that *Parade* magazine, the studies showing that

- Watching too much TV kills brain cells, resulting in lethargy, dullness, and robot-like passiveness.
- Sixteen percent of kids under twelve are obese and diabetic because of crunching and munching while watching hours of TV.
- Adult obesity is epidemic, largely because of watching TV.

Those addicted to TV find themselves drugged into thinking

- There are no solutions, only problems, problems, problems.
- Their wives or husbands should look like the super babes or sexy hunks on TV.
- That it's cool to cut family members, mock fellow employees, disrespect the cops, kick at the rules, and rant and rave to get your way.

Remind me, Lord, that for generations we existed without TV.

Teach. Read. Walk. Sleep. Pray. Sing. Dance. Play games. Visit a neighbor. Visit a hospital.

Married? Make love.

Help me, Lord, to keep in front of me my awkward acronym:

T	There is
A	Always
S	Something
B	Better
T	To
D	Do than
W	Watch
T	T
V	V

Burning to be or not to be.

I want TO BE alert, loving, successful, energetic, and alive. So, if the question is "TV or no TV," the answer is, "No TV."

Because I want to BE.

And, thank you, Lord, for reminding me that when I am watching TV, I am watching <u>someone else fulfill *their* goals</u>. Better to use that time to fulfill MY goals.

(Ya' know, Lord, everything I said about TV also applies to the Internet. Big time thief. Big family thief.) Help us all, Lord. Amen.

The Flame:

What goes into someone's mouth does not defile them, but what comes out of their mouth, that is what defiles them.

Matthew 15:11

I will not look with approval on anything that is vile. I hate what faithless people do; I will have no part in it.

Psalm 101:3

FIRE IT UP!

This is how I am burning "to be" with no TV:

_____

_____

_____

_____

_____

_____

_____

_____

My Passionate Prayer Time:

_____

_____

_____

_____

_____

_____

_____

_____

_____

63

Burning for the Bible

You've heard me say it, Lord, on my radio show and in public forums: "I'll give $1,000 to anyone who can show me in
the Constitution where it says separation of church and state is
mandated in our country."

I've still got my thousand bucks.

Separation of church and state is not in the Constitution,
and it's not in our national documents, which you helped us
frame, Lord.

And I'm not the only one who has raised this challenge,
am I? In my interview with lawyer/writer Ann Coulter, she
stated that she had challenged law professors to locate in the
Constitution any reference to separation of church and state.
She still has HER thousand bucks.

That's one reason to bring the Bible back into classroom,
courtroom, and Congress, isn't it?

And it's legal, loving, and long overdue.

There it is, Lord—the three reasons I am burning for the Bible to be back in the classroom, courtroom, and Congress.

Legal, loving, and long overdue.

LEGAL. You were there at the beginning, Lord, when those early settlers set foot on America's soil. While the *Mayflower* was still swaying and rocking in Cape Cod Bay, they wrote The Mayflower Compact:

> In the name of God, Amen. We whose names are underwritten, the loyal subjects of our dread Sovereign Lord King James, by the Grace of God of Great Britain, France, and Ireland, King, defender of the Faith, etc.
>
> Having undertaken, for the Glory of God and advancements of the Christian faith and honor of our King and Country, a voyage to plant the first colony in the Northern Parts of Virginia, do by these presents, solemnly and mutually, in the presence of God, and one another, covenant and combine ourselves together into a civil body politic; for our better ordering, and preservation and furtherance of the ends aforesaid; and by virtue hereof to enact, constitute and frame, such just and equal laws, ordinances, acts, constitutions and offices, from

time to time, as shall be thought most meet and convenient for the general good of the colony; unto which we promise all due submission and obedience.

In witness whereof we have hereunto subscribed our names at Cape Cod the 11th of November, in the year of the reign of our Sovereign Lord King James, of England, France, and Ireland, the eighteenth, and of Scotland the fifty-fourth, 1620.

And then one hundred and fifty years later, Lord, came the affirmations, which we examined earlier:

Again, GEORGE WASHINGTON:

"It is the duty of nations to acknowledge the progress of Almighty God, to obey His will, to be grateful for His benefits and humbly to implore His protection and favor."

Again, BENJAMIN FRANKLIN:

". . . God works in the affairs of men. . . . We have been assured, in the Sacred Writings that 'except the Lord build the House, they labor in vain that build it.' I firmly believe this."

Again, THOMAS JEFFERSON:

> "We hold these truths to be self-evident, that all men (and women) are created equal, that they are endowed by <u>THEIR CREATOR</u> with certain inalienable rights, that among these are life, liberty and the pursuit of happiness."

I am burning to bring the Bible back into the classroom, courtroom, and Congress, Lord, because it is legal. I will not let others steal our national and sacred heritage. Common sense and early American law recognized that there has to be a law above human law and that law above human law is your Word, Lord.

It's LOVING.

How would it be, Lord, to have visible over the teacher's right shoulder your commands?

THE TEN COMMANDMENTS

"You shall have no other gods before me.

> *"You shall not make for yourself an image in the form of anything in heaven above or on the earth beneath or in the waters below. You shall not bow down to them or worship them; for I, the Lord your God, am a jealous God, punishing the children for the sin of the parents to the third*

and fourth generation of those who hate me, but showing love to a thousand generations of those who love me and keep my commandments.

"You shall not misuse the name of the Lord your God, for the Lord will not hold anyone guiltless who misuses his name.

"Remember the Sabbath day by keeping it holy. Six days you shall labor and do all your work, but the seventh day is a sabbath to the Lord your God. On it you shall not do any work, neither you, nor your son or daughter, nor your male or female servant, nor your animals, nor any foreigner residing in your towns. For in six days the Lord made the heavens and the earth, the sea, and all that is in them, but he rested on the seventh day. Therefore the Lord blessed the Sabbath day and made it holy.

"Honor your father and your mother, so that you may live long in the land the Lord your God is giving you.

"You shall not murder.

"You shall not commit adultery.

"You shall not steal.

"You shall not give false testimony against your neighbor.

"You shall not covet your neighbor's house. You shall not covet your neighbor's wife, or his male or female servant, his ox or donkey, or anything that belongs to your neighbor."

Exodus 20:3–17

And over the teacher's left shoulder:

THE BEATITUDES

Blessed are the poor in spirit, for theirs is the kingdom of heaven.

Blessed are those who mourn, for they will be comforted.

Blessed are the meek, for they will inherit the earth.

Blessed are those who hunger and thirst for righteousness, for they will be filled.

Blessed are the merciful, for they will be shown mercy.

Blessed are the pure in heart, for they will see God.

Blessed are the peacemakers, for they will be called children of God.

Blessed are those who are persecuted because of righteousness, for theirs is the kingdom of heaven.

Blessed are you when people insult you, persecute you and falsely say all kinds of evil against you because of me. Rejoice and be glad, because great is your reward in heaven, for in the same way they persecuted the prophets who were before you.

And right smack in the middle of the room, flashing from the center of the teacher's desk

THE FRUIT OF THE SPIRIT

The fruit of the Spirit is
love, joy, peace, forbearance,
kindness, goodness, faithfulness, self-control.

The teacher wouldn't have to say a word.

Grace, courtesy, and love would permeate the room all day long if you and your Word were embraced and obeyed.

And students would feel good about themselves.

Rather than

- Students spraying the halls with bullets.
- Students committing suicide because of bullying.
- Sixteen-year-olds bragging how rapidly they can get pregnant.
- Students hustling drugs at their lockers.
- Students ganging up on their teachers.

Rather than these brutalities, there would be healthy attitudes. Respect, discipline, courtesy, purity, friendliness, self-control, and compassion would gradually arise and permeate the room, halls, and building like the scent of fresh flowers. It frankly wouldn't matter if the halls were filled with Muslims, Buddhists, Baptists, Atheists, or any religious groupings—the beautiful scent of these "fresh flowers" would be enjoyed by everyone.

It would be smart, healthy, and loving to fill the entire atmosphere of the school with your grace, power, and compassion. All would benefit.

Your Word says, "Mightier is the man who conquers his spirit than he who conquers a city." The passions of a youthful spirit would be encircled by a ring of divine love and self-control.

And it's LONG OVERDUE, Lord, for students to feel that level of Godly discipline and healthy self-control. Lord, you know that public schools and universities are rotting from within. Who knows whether there's a decade left or two decades left before society collapses into social and economic chaos and moral and spiritual decay? Just like ancient Rome, Lord.

Dr. Bruce Shortt calls our schools "pagan seminaries."

"If it feels good to you, just do it! Do what you like!" That's the daily lesson.

The mantra at public schools is like the one flashing in front of Central High: "Central School District is dedicated to helping every student fulfill whatever he or she thinks is best." What THEY think is best? Become a bookie? Druggie? Charles Manson? Bernie Madoff? A hooker?

Fuggedaboutit.

If education is the cradle of civilization, then bad education has got to be the coffin of civilization. That's tough for me to say, Lord. You know how much I loved being a teacher, seeing students learn and grow. You know how much I loved seeing my students KNOW that they were taught by someone who cared for them and not just someone who insisted they memorize Shakespeare or work quadratic equations.

I know the question will be asked: Do ethics need to be taught in schools? And here, Lord, I am not talking about thin platitudes and meaningless phrases like: "Be nice to everyone" or "Just don't offend anyone."

In the absence of firm ethical standards, we now have a nation of Adam Wheelers. *Conning Harvard* is the story of Adam Wheeler who, over a period of six years, tricked the smartest institutions in the country time and time again.

Adam Wheeler was an expert forger and a skillful liar with seemingly few scruples about fabricating his academic credentials. In snagging admission to Harvard, he unfairly attained an honor that millions of students worldwide dream of achieving legitimately. In conning several institutions at the pinnacle of higher education—Yale, Brown, Stanford, the Rhodes and Fulbright scholarships, and more—he astonished the nation with the story of his audacity and blatant absence of morality.

Eventually Adam Wheeler got caught.

Frank Abagnale Jr., author of *Catch Me If You Can*, summed it up well: "*Conning Harvard* proves that what I did over forty years ago [in deceiving people] is four thousand times easier to do today due to technology. Technology breeds crime and makes replicating documents and falsifying paper child's play. This, added with the fact that we live in an extremely unethical society that doesn't teach ethics at home and doesn't teach ethics at school because the teacher would be accused of teaching morality, has brought us to a country full of Adam Wheelers. For those who are naïve, a must read."

The classroom (again) then the courtroom (again) and then Congress (again).

Classroom, Courtroom, Congress

They are all under your loving authority, Lord.

God bless America, land that I love. Amen.

PS. Lord, did you catch that documentary on PBS about "America's Godly Heritage"? Just fifty or sixty years ago, the President, John F. Kennedy, said, ". . . the rights of man come not from the generosity of the state, but from the hand of God."

And decades later, Representative Dick Armey led a prayer on television, following the 9/11 massacre. He gathered Congress together on the Capitol steps in front of a national audience to lead a series of prayers and a loud chorus of "God Bless America."

And they sang, and they sang, and they sang.

It's too bad it took the tragedy of 9/11 for a nation to proclaim your sovereignty, Lord. It's too bad it took the tragedy of 9/11 to bring us together again under your grace and power. Shed your grace upon us again, Lord. For your glory. Amen.

The Flame:

If my people, who are called by my name, will humble themselves and pray and seek my face and turn from their wicked ways, then I will hear from heaven and I will forgive their sin and will heal their land.

2 Chronicles 7:14

In those days Israel had no king; everyone did as he saw fit.

Judges 21:24

FIRE IT UP!

This is how I help to bring the Bible back to the classroom, the courtroom, and the Congress:

_____

_____

_____

_____

_____

_____

_____

_____

My Passionate Prayer Time:

_____

_____

_____

_____

_____

_____

_____

_____

Epilogue

A Passionate Beginning: A New Starting Point

Y ou got this far. So you're clearly a man who is passionate about honoring God, improving yourself, rescuing people, enriching your family, and fighting for America.

"Let's roll."

It's time for action.

We've long been motivated by slogans like "Remember the Alamo," "Remember Pearl Harbor," "Remember 9/11," and "What Would Jesus Do?" These slogans remind us that our passion for God and people and our country is right on target.

Some guys have lost hope and given up.

Not you.

On the back of a dollar bill is a picture of an unfinished pyramid with an eye above it. Our early government leaders wanted us to continue building our families and our nation under the watchful "eye of God."

Under the pyramid is a Latin phrase that means, "He has smiled on our undertaking!"

You and I are God's men and God's leaders. Burning for, praying for, and acting on behalf of the NEXT great awakening.

The first Great Awakening revival in the 1730s and 1740s witnessed thousands of our American ancestors giving their lives to Jesus Christ. It was one of the biggest reasons America emerged as a Christian nation.

Men, we will unite again.

This is the time; this is the place.

And you are the man.

Let's roll.

About the Author

W. Neil Gallagher, PhD is a financial journalist, investment educator, and seasoned broadcaster. As the host of "Family and Financial Fitness," Dr. Gallagher has fielded thousands of questions related to financial communication, estate planning, wealth creation, family enrichment, and the psychology of investing. Author of *The Money Doctor's Guide to Taking Care of Yourself When No One Else Will*, Dr. Gallagher is the financial speaker for Zig Ziglar's *Born to Win* seminars. Having conducted hundreds of programs for employees and retirees of several Fortune 500 companies, Dr. Gallagher maintains a private practice of individual and institutional clients totaling one billion dollars.

Gallagher earned a doctorate from Brown University and is the author of five books and seventy popular and scholarly articles in publications such as the *Journal of Value Inquiry*, *Charisma/ Christian Life*, *World Vision*, and *Bottom Line* magazine.